This book is about the German U-boats and the men who lived, fought, and died in them. Over 39,000 officers and men served in the German submarine fleet—all but 7,000 of them found an ocean grave.

Harald Busch was attached to the U-boat branch of the Kriegsmarine and shared in many of the battles and patrols he describes. He tells with the vividness of personal experience exactly what it was like to lie in wait for a convoy at dawn—and how it feels to sweat out twenty-four hours on the bottom of the ocean, when the lights have gone out and the water is rising over the engines . . . and the next depth charge may crush the hull.

From the easy "kills" of the war's first days to the last desperate patrols, this is the story—told by an insider—of German U-boats at war . . . a war they almost won.

More War Library titles
Published by Ballantine Books:

THE BURNING OF THE SHIPS
by Douglas Scott

INSIDE THE SAS
by Tony Geraghty

SHARKS AND LITTLE FISH
by Wolfgang Ott

NO MAN'S LAND
by John Toland

KAMIKAZE
by Yasuo Kuwahara and Gordon T. Allred

AIRCRAFT CARRIER
by Joseph Bryan III

U-BOATS
AT WAR

Harald Busch

Translated from the German by

L. P. R. Wilson

BALLANTINE BOOKS • NEW YORK

CONTENTS

Preface

THIS BOOK is about the German U-boats and the men who lived, fought and died in them in the tragedy of the greatest war in history. Over 39,000 officers and men served in 820 submarines—all but 7,000 of them found an ocean grave. From first to last, they fought against steadily mounting odds and, in this sense, their achievement was unique among feats of German arms.

Much has been written about the U-boat war, from the officially inspired wartime accounts to the superficial surveys, inaccurate, sometimes to the point of deliberate distortion, of the postwar years. All too often, the writers' preconceived ideas have obscured the essential features of their subject. Descriptions of successful U-boat commanders being welcomed home with garlands of oak leaves and oceans of flowers are as misleading as talk of brutal U-boat men shooting at struggling survivors. The truth is, those who fought in the U-boat service were neither heroes nor war criminals.

By now, after ten years, the passions of war have cooled and emotional bias yields to a more detached attitude, in which an attempt can be made to measure the achievements of German U-boat crews in the late war by the standards and traditions of their service. I hope that this book may help to foster this more objective approach. It represents an attempt to depict what the U-boat war meant to the handful of men engaged in it.

Being attached to the U-boat branch of the Kriegsmarine, I was able to share in the battles and the atmosphere of those times, and the scenes portrayed in this book are based on personal experience, as well as on conversations with my former comrades and on descriptions furnished by former U-boat commanders and their men. Their accounts I have carefully checked by comparing them with the records preserved in the war diaries of the U-boats concerned. I have also taken into consideration such relevant material on the U-boat war as has become available from responsible sources, both German and British.

The events so baldly and unemotionally set down in the war diaries, I have attempted to re-create, instilling into them, from my own experience, as much as I could of their original urgency and of the atmosphere peculiar to those times. That it was certain particular U-boats and not others whose operations I have chosen to describe has been due solely to the limitations of my own experience and to the inevitable element of chance in the collection of the necessary material.

The achievements in the early, successful phases of the U-boat war naturally lend themselves to a broader and more arresting treatment than the many less fruitful actions carried out in the later stages by men who have remained unknown to the general public. Nevertheless, I believe that for sheer skill and endurance not a few of these nameless deeds deserve equal if not greater recognition than the feats of the "Aces" in the heyday of the U-boat war.

It may well be doubted whether sufficient reliable material, from official and other sources, is yet available to justify an attempt to write a definitive history of U-boat operations from 1939 to 1945. I would stress that such has in no way been my intention. What follows springs simply from the desire to convey, within the essential historical and technical framework, something of the duties and of the spirit of that small élite who served in German U-boats—and to serve was indeed their highest aim. May this account of their exploits help their fellow-countrymen to preserve undimmed the memory of the fallen, and find inspiration in their example, at a time when Germany is struggling for survival as a nation.

Life in a U-Boat

To THOSE who have never been to sea in a submarine, it is hard indeed to convey an adequate idea of what it means to live, sometimes for months on end, in a narrow tubular space amid foul air and universal damp. Yet once they had learned to accept it and had become constitutionally adapted, the U-boat men were no longer irked by their unnatural environment and were able even to feel at home in it, while those whose first experience of a U-boat was to accompany one on an offensive patrol (as was the case with the present author) were surprised to find themselves taking the daily routine more and more as a matter of course until finally, like real submariners, they came to look on voyaging below the surface of the sea as the most intimate and impressive of all forms of ocean travel.

For their duties on board, the U-boat crews were divided into three watches, each of four hours, with the exception of the engine-room ratings, who were in two watches of six hours. The men, therefore, slept in shifts. But undressing while at sea was out of the question, for the U-boat might attack or be attacked at any moment of the day or night and then the entire crew, averaging forty-six men, would turn out, each to his special task at his special post.

A U-boat would set off on patrol loaded with supplies to last several weeks in a quantity certainly never intended by the designers, and the space available to the crew, already small in German operational boats, would be reduced to minute proportions. Fresh food, for consumption early in the voyage, was so bulky that movement was almost impossible in the compartments where it was stowed.

Throughout the U-boat the air would be heavy with odors —the penetrating, dungeon-smell from the bilges, the whiff of Diesel oil and of unwashed humanity, the smell of cooking, of "Colibri" (eau-de-Cologne used by the crew to remove the salt encrusted on their faces by the seas which broke continuously over the bridge) and a generous contribution, despite air purifier, from the direction of a door on overworked hinges, where seldom indeed was the blue light not shining that signified "engaged."

And always when at sea the submarine would be in motion, violent motion — corkscrewing, pitching, yawing, rolling, adapting herself to the surge and swell of the water. In heavy seas the ship would not infrequently heel through an angle of almost sixty degrees; sometimes a sleeper would be catapulted out of his bunk—they were built lengthways into the sides of the hull—and awake to find himself on the deck. It has happened that a man would be shot straight from an upper berth into the lower berth on the opposite side of the boat.

In the U-boats employed during the war, the seamen's mess was in the torpedo-stowage compartment. Until the first torpedo had been fired and the first reload hoisted into the empty tube, there was no room to stand upright or to sit down in the normal way, for an additional number of reload torpedoes were stowed at the usual deck-level and the crew were accommodated on a temporary deck built of wooden planking above them. Even this space was cluttered, like the rest of the boat, with hampers, crates and sacks of food, while overhead swung hammocks stuffed to bursting with further provisions and supplies.

The petty-officers' mess, situated immediately abaft the control-room, (the brain- and nerve-center of the U-boat) was equally cramped. The narrow central gangway between the tiers of bunks was completely filled by a mess-table running the whole length of the compartment, and the flap which comprised a third of its width had therefore always to be left down, or there would have been no room to pass through. Beneath the table were stowed more sacks of provisions, probably potatoes, and above, almost at head level, hung hammocks full of "Kommissbrot," the hard navy bread.

Most of the traffic of the boat went through the P.O.s' mess (we called it the "Leipzigerstrasse"), and anyone wishing to pass from the control-room to the galley, the engine-room or the after torpedo compartment had literally to scramble and squirm his way past these obstacles. When off duty, the men had perforce to lie on their bunks. Sitting was less popular, as it necessitated cramping the legs by dangling them over the side of the safety-board and moreover in this position, when-over the relieving of the watch turned the P.O.s' mess into a main thoroughfare (which invariably happened at mealtimes) it was necessary for the occupant of the bunk to retract his head beneath the low mattress of the bunk above, at the same time drawing in his knees and feet, before anyone could negotiate the narrow and treacherous route between table and bunks, menaced by loaves of bread from above and sacks of potatoes from below.

Yet all this was worth while if the patrol was successful. By far the greatest strain on the crew was to be keyed up for action at any moment and then, after days and weeks spent in these cramped and exacting conditions, not to meet with the enemy, for without even the opportunity of a successful action, all their efforts and endurance would have seemed in vain. It was in such circumstances that nervous breakdowns were most likely to occur, entailing sooner or later the release of the men concerned from sea-going service. But such cases were never numerous among U-boat crews, for the majority of those who proved physically or temperamentally unsuited to the life were quickly spotted and transferred to other duties.

In the late war, a great deal was done for the U-boat men, and rightly. They were given the best possible rations. When a U-boat was in dock being overhauled for its next patrol, the majority of the crew were given home leave. The remainder, if they were not required to work on the boat, were sent to one of the special rest camps that were set up in the neighborhood of all U-boat bases. At the beginning of the war, members of crews were withdrawn from service, protest though they might, after twelve patrols; but from 1943, few U-boats survived their second, and for many of them the first patrol proved also to be their last.

Nevertheless, throughout the war, U-boat volunteers were never lacking, even in the seemingly hopeless period in 1943-44, while the disaffection rumored and "revealed" in the postwar press—it was said, for example, that one U-boat commander and even the whole of his crew had refused to go on patrol—never, in fact, existed. Indeed, in *The Battle of the Atlantic*, published in 1946, the British Admiralty paid the following tribute to the men of the U-boats:

". . . there is no reason to suppose that they would not have fought in a losing campaign, if the defeat of the German Army had not brought collapse and surrender. Their morale was unimpaired to the bitter end."

The loss of 783 German submarines and 32,000 men out of a total sea-going strength of 39,000 speaks for itself. Surely no other branch of the armed forces has ever suffered such casualties in war — and survived without serious effects on morale. Certainly none has achieved such large-scale and far-reaching results with so comparatively few men and materials.

PART I

SEPTEMBER 3, 1939—SUMMER, 1940

The Battle Reviewed

AT THE outbreak of war, on September 3, 1939, Germany possessed only 57 U-boats, of which no more than 22 were of a size suitable for operations in the Atlantic (Type IX of 740 tons and Type VII of 517 tons). The remainder were all of Type II, the so-called "Dugouts" of 250 tons, with which Germany had begun in 1935 to form the basis of her new submarine force. These were intended for coastal work, for training rather than for operational use.

As the disparity in naval strengths was too great to allow of a direct challenge to British sea power, the German Naval Command realized that a decision against Britain would have to be sought by other means and, if possible, forced before the threat of United States intervention could be fulfilled.

In 1939, therefore, in contrast to the endless vacillations of the first world war, policy in regard to the employment of U-boats was clear from the start. Attacks on enemy merchant shipping were to begin at once and with all available means and were confidently expected to achieve a sharp constriction of Britain's vital supplies.

THE SINKING OF THE *Athenia*

September 3, 1939, found the U-boats at sea and ready to go into action. Hardly had they been informed of the British declaration of war than Oberleutnant Lemp, commanding U.30, sighted a passenger liner on a bearing favorable for torpedo attack. As the liner was off the normal shipping route and moreover was zigzagging, he took it for a troopship and, establishing its British nationality, accordingly attacked. The ship, the *Athenia*, with passengers bound from England for the United States, was sunk with the loss of 128 lives.

This unfortunate mistake had fateful consequences, for it presented the British government with the opportunity to assert that from the very first day of hostilities Germany had waged unrestricted U-boat warfare and despite the fact that the strictly legal conduct of all other U-boats soon disproved this allegation, Britain adhered to the charge and repeated it in justification of her own breaches of international law.

The German government immediately denied the charge and further, denied that the *Athenia* had been sunk by a German U-boat. At the time, the disclaimer was made in good faith, for none of the patrolling U-boats had reported the incident, while all had received strict instructions to treat merchant shipping in accordance with Prize Regulations.

Meanwhile, well realizing the probable consequences of his action, Oberleutnant Lemp made no mention of it in his wireless reports, and it was only when the U.30 returned to base at the end of September that he informed Dönitz verbally that it was he who had sunk the *Athenia*.

But instead of then admitting the mistake and expressing regret, the German government continued to deny all responsibility and instructed the Naval High Command to insure that the matter was kept strictly secret. Kommodore Dönitz had therefore no alternative but to order Lemp to remove the offending page from the war diary of the U.30 and substitute another page in which the record of the sinking was omitted, so that the truth should not leak out when the customary eight copies of the war diary were prepared.

Though the war diaries were secret, they were open to scrutiny for training purposes (as the number of copies indicates), so that the suppression of the *Athenia* incident, ordered by the highest political and military authorities, could not be insured by any other means. The whole matter was closely investigated by the Nürnberg tribunal. It remains the only recorded instance of a subsequent alteration in a U-boat's war diary.

But the Reich propaganda ministry carried the matter a step further and, without informing the naval high command of its intention, put out the abstruse assertion that the sinking of the *Athenia* was brought about by the explosion of an infernal machine, placed in the ship on the instructions of the First Lord of the Admiralty, Mr. Winston Churchill, in order that credence might be lent to the charge that it was Germany that had first broken the rules of sea warfare!

A direct consequence of the *Athenia* incident, of far-reaching effect on the whole of the first phase of the U-boat war, was the order that in future no passenger ships, whatever their nationality, were to be sunk, whether in enemy service or not, whether sailing alone or in convoy. To this restriction of the U-boat's freedom of action and their prospects of success was soon to be added another. It being considered desirable that Germany should not fire the first shot in hostilities with France, the U-boats were forbidden to attack French ships.

The severity of the restrictions which these orders placed on U-boat operations can readily be understood when it is remembered, firstly, that they were in force at the time the British Expeditionary Force was transferred to France, when U-boats were still able to operate in the Channel and, secondly, that at night it is impossible to determine a ship's nationality. The second order was only rescinded on November 24, 1939, while the first, forbidding the sinking of passenger ships, remained in force into the summer of 1940.

BLOCKADE AND COUNTER-BLOCKADE

From the earliest days of hostilities, the U-boat war on merchant shipping, the "Supply War," as it has been called, was prosecuted in answer to the British blockade of Germany. Immediately war broke out, Britain had published a comprehensive contraband list. A few days later, Germany issued a similar list, but whereas Britain's control of the adjacent seas enabled her to enforce the inspection of neutral cargoes in her own harbors, Germany could only prosecute the counter-blockade with U-boats that intercepted ships on the high seas and took their cargoes in prize, with occasional commerce raiders and with mine-laying, principally by U-boats and aircraft.

On November 27, 1939, Britain extended her blockade of Germany by imposing an absolute ban on the importation of German goods by neutrals, introducing, in order to enforce this, the Navicert System and setting up a British supervising authority in the neutral states themselves to control the whole of their trade.

It was naturally claimed for these measures that, though damaging to the trade and perhaps infringing the rights of the neutrals, they did not endanger their ships or their seamen and therefore represented a more humane method of waging war than the taking of prizes upon the high seas. But in practice the very necessity of reporting at certain British control points exposed neutral ships and their crews to the risk of destruction, for the minefields intended to protect the specified approaches to the harbors concerned along the British coasts proved inadequate for the purpose, and Germany saw herself justified in concentrating her attacks and in mining the fairway on precisely those routes which neutral shipping was obliged to follow.

From the first day of the war, British merchant shipping had been placed under Admiralty instructions, thereby forgoing the rights to which it would have been entitled under international law. Moreover, the ships were armed, not only with guns for self-defense (in British eyes, a legitimate precaution), but also with depth-charges, for the purpose of destroying U-boats. The faster ships, at first not sailing in convoy, were equipped, in addition, with special depth-charge throwers and with Asdic, so that the distinction between offensive and defensive weapons, for which Britain had constantly pressed before the war but which had never officially been defined, now ceased to exist altogether.

As further indication of their belligerent role, British merchant ships were ordered to be blacked out at night, to report immediately by wireless the position of any U-boat encountered, and finally as Churchill announced on October 1, 1939, their captains were instructed to ram all U-boats on sight. Thereupon, German U-boats were instructed that they might in future attack without warning any merchant ship that was definitely seen to be armed. On October 17 an amendment to this instruction was issued, substituting "any enemy merchant ship" and omitting the qualification concerning armament.

Thus U-boats were now no longer exposed to attack by "tramp steamers" with concealed batteries of guns, the U-boat traps or "Q-ships" of the first world war.

There remained the question of neutral ships with cargoes bound for Britain. For a U-boat to surface, challenge them and carry out a search for contraband was becoming an extremely difficult and dangerous operation, at any rate in the coastal areas where the concentrations of ships made them easier to intercept, and before the war at sea had lasted a month—on September 30, 1939—this procedure had to be abandoned.

Shortly afterward, on January 6, 1940, following the example of President Roosevelt's Pan-American Security Zone, Germany defined certain "operational areas," in which any shipping encountered was liable to be sunk at sight. The first of these included the sea areas off the Shetland and Orkney Islands and the east coast of Scotland.

Keeping pace, however, with the extension of U-boat operations, was the increasing effectiveness of British defense. Existing technical devices were improved and new ones made their appearance, while an ever-growing number of vessels with specially trained crews were devoted to anti-U-boat duties. In these, according to British statements, Captain F. J. Walker, R.N.,[1] who died in 1944, performed outstanding services. But not only the sloops and other U-boat chasers, but also the escort vessels—cruisers, destroyers and, later, corvettes and frigates—and the merchant ships themselves became continually more skillful in evading the U-boats and defending themselves when attacked.

Thus the task of the U-boats became progressively more dangerous and more exacting, demanding ever higher standards of skill and daring from each individual commander. Their most dangerous foe was the aircraft. At first, the only planes to appear over the sea were the unwieldy Sunderland flying-boats and it was nearly always possible to evade them by promptly submerging. Then, in addition to aircraft carriers, freighters and escorting cruisers began to be fitted with aircraft-launching devices until finally, with its fast, shore-based planes of modern design and with a range of at least 600 miles, the British Coastal Command became the U-boats' Enemy Number One.

[1] Captain F. J. Walker, R.N., C.B., D.S.O. (3 bars), as commander of two Escort Groups, destroyed over 30 U-boats. The outstanding exponent of offensive tactics in convoy protection.—*Translator*.

MINE-LAYING

Apart from the isolated achievements of U-boats in sinking enemy warships and their pressure on the supply routes to Britain, astoundingly successful results were obtained in the first few months of the war, before the declaration of German operational areas, from mine-laying. In this work, as it did not entail long periods at sea, the small, costal Type II U-boats of 250 tons could be employed, each carrying six to eight mines in place of the usual torpedoes.

The principal areas mined were, to the west, the northern and southern passages between Britain and Ireland (North Channel and St. George's Channel), the Firth of Clyde and the approaches to the English Channel, and, to the east, the narrow shipping route off the English coast protected on its seaward side by minefields and especially the Thames and Tyne estuaries. Breaking through the inadequate defenses, the U-boats were able to lay their mines in the middle of the shipping lanes, preferably in the narrowest places, or near the approach buoys and, if possible, in the harbor mouths themselves.

It was not unusual for fifty per cent of these mines to find their target, six mines, for example, damaging or even sinking three vessels in quick succession—an unbelievably high proportion. It was during this period that Kapitänleutnant Schepke acquired among his comrades the nickname of "Passepartout" Schepke, because with perhaps more daring than most he succeeded in his U-boat in laying mines at the most sensitive points in the network of the enemy's sea communications.

These mine-laying operations were carried out with extraordinarily small losses, but as a result Britain was compelled to undertake repeated sweeps of the allegedly safe passages now crowded with shipping, where despite the efforts to clear the mines, repeated losses occurred, provoking neutral protests.

At first the enemy was mystified by the new type of magnetic mine, but the principle upon which it worked was soon discovered and counter-measures were rapidly introduced. To these we shall return later.

THE NEW U-BOAT STRATEGY

For a time the magnetic mine remained Germany's most
effective weapon in prosecuting the blockade of Britain, until
three main factors combined to alter the whole scope and
strategy of the U-boat war.

The most important of these was the fall of France and the
occupation by Germany of the French ports from Dunkirk
to Bordeaux, compelling Britain to gather together into one
main sea-artery between the north of Ireland and the west of
Scotland the overseas traffic that had previously used the
widely dispersed approaches of the English Channel and the
Bristol and St. George's Channels. At the same time, British
coastal areas, including those off the western coast of Scotland, were being increasingly well protected by aircraft.
Finally, the definition by Germany of operational areas where
enemy or enemy-controlled shipping would be sunk without
warning gave the U-boats a new freedom of action in that
they could now attack by day or by night on the surface or
when submerged.

The first factor moved the center of gravity of the enemy's
shipping movements farther north, the second, that of U-boat
operations farther west, while the de-restriction of U-boat
warfare enabled Kommodore Dönitz to put into practice
against the North Atlantic convoys the tactics which he had
devised and rehearsed with his crews before the war. Hence-
forth, in contrast with the early months of the war, when
according to British statements 97 per cent of all merchant
shipping losses had taken place during the hours of daylight,
the U-boats attacked at night and on the surface, thereby
minimizing the dangers of pursuit by an enemy equipped with
Asdics, hydrophones and depth charges.

FAULTY GERMAN TORPEDOES

U-boat commanders experienced from the very start a high
proportion of failures in torpedo attacks, even in circumstances when it seemed impossible to miss the target. The
reason was not far to seek: the German torpedoes were defective.

The commanders themselves had often had cause to suspect that this was the case, but their complaints had always met with an official answer to the effect that "the negative results obtained would appear to have been due to inaccurate setting of the magnetic firing pistol, through failure on the part of those responsible to take into account the variation required in the setting, according to the position of the submarine at the time of firing in relation to the magnetic pole." Now, it transpired that the U-boat commanders had been right after all.

Besides the so-called A-torpedo, driven by compressed air, which was still used at long ranges and in night attacks, the electrically propelled E-torpedo (already appearing toward the end of the first world war) was put into service on the outbreak of hostilities. Whereas the former left a visible track of air bubbles, revealing the source of discharge and if spotted in time enabling the target to take avoiding action, the E-torpedo left no trace of its passage through the water and, when fired by the recently developed method of "surgeless" discharge, had the advantage of complete surprise.

But in these torpedoes the contact type of fuse, mounted in the warhead, had largely been replaced by a newly developed magnetic proximity fuse, actuated on coming within a ship's magnetic field and set to explode when at the most effective distance beneath the hull.

The advantages of such a fuse are obvious, for instead of firing the charge upon contact with the side of the ship, it now exploded the torpedo some distance below the keel, thus breaking the back of the ship and sinking it with greater certainty and in a shorter space of time.

But the magnetic proximity fuse proved unreliable, firing the charge too soon or too late and sometimes not at all, while the E-torpedoes often failed to run at the depth for which they had been set. The principal factor in the failure of so many torpedoes to find their targets, however, was the measures taken by the enemy to counter the magnetic mine, of which the German naval command was at that time unaware.

In order to reduce the strength of the magnetic field that permanently surrounds a ship's hull, the British had resorted to electric cables, through which a current was passed supplied by the ship's generators, wound horizontally round the hull—"Degaussing"—or, alternatively, to discharging a powerful current, again through a cable, round the sides of the ship at periodic intervals—"Wiping." Both methods reduced the ship's magnetic field sufficiently to render the magnetic fuse of a torpedo ineffective.

Whatever the relative importance of these various factors in affecting the German torpedoes, the British battleship *Warspite* was attacked no less than five times at Narvik in the most favorable conditions and each time the torpedoes missed their target.

In another patrol, during November and December 1939, Prien suffered six torpedo failures. Other U-boats had similar experiences. The commanders returning from the Norwegian campaign therefore used blunt language when making the usual verbal report to Dönitz, till the latter demanded categorically of the authorities concerned that the source of the defect of the faulty torpedoes must be established without delay and the trouble finally cured.

The Torpedo School accordingly set to work to trace the defect, and, meanwhile, the magnetic fuse was abandoned and the old contact fuse restored. Even then the torpedoes often failed to strike their target and it was discovered that, apart from the unsatisfactory magnetic pistol, the type of depth-setting gear incorporated in the torpedoes themselves was faulty.

The seriousness of this discovery can be judged by the fact that to inflict the maximum damage it is particularly important for a torpedo to strike its target at the greatest possible depth below the waterline. Any error, therefore, in the depth-setter might result in failure to sink the ship or as often as not in failure to hit it at all.

Until the summer of 1941, when this defect and that of the magnetic firing-pistol were finally cured, U-boat commanders had to make do with the existing E-torpedoes fitted with the contact pistol. Experience soon brought to light a yet further difficulty.

In peace time practice firing, recently manufactured torpedoes had always been used and the question of their storage life had not arisen, but now it was found that, after lying for some weeks in a patrolling U-boat, their functioning was still further impaired. To U-boat commanders' existing burdens was therefore added the task of regulating periodically all torpedo mechanisms. In the case of torpedoes already loaded into the tubes, this involved withdrawing them to three-quarters of their length, charging their batteries and checking the accuracy of their instruments once every forty-eight hours.

Though these measures helped to reduce the number of torpedo failures due to premature or delayed firing of the charge, the premature explosion of a torpedo fired by U.39 at the aircraft carrier, *Ark Royal*, 150 miles west of the Hebrides, was responsible, on September 14, 1939, for the first U-boat loss of the war.

Size and Achievement of the U-boat Force

In the period between the outbreak of war and the conversion of French Atlantic harbors into U-boat bases in the late summer of 1940, new-construction failed to keep pace with losses and the total number of U-boats available for service therefore continually decreased. In the same period, the number of boats actually on patrol averaged between three and five, while for a few days over Christmas, 1940, only one boat was at sea, the remainder being either in dock or engaged on training duties. From the spring of 1941 to the end of that year, the number of patrolling U-boats increased by ten per month, thereafter by twenty per month and more.

Nevertheless, by the summer of 1940, a total of 2½ million gross register tons of shipping had been sunk for the loss of seven U-boats—a considerable achievement. The accuracy of the first figure is confirmed by the almost identical figure of tonnage sunk which has been published since the war in Britain and is evidence of the scrupulous care taken by U-boat commanders (as distinct from Luftwaffe pilots on similar occasions) in compiling their reports.

When operating later in the war in Mid or South Atlantic, where ships were frequently encountered traveling without escort and unarmed, commanders were nearly always able to identify the vessel attacked and stay surfaced until its sinking could be observed, but in less remote areas this was not the case and they were then faced with the difficulty of assessing the tonnage of a ship seen only as a shadow at night and of predicting its fate by what could be seen of the place and manner of the explosion and of the behavior of the ship in the few moments before the U-boat submerged. In these circumstances, the accuracy of the figure of tonnage claimed as destroyed is truly astounding.

Fighting Patrols

1 A FEAT OF ARMS

IF THE first successful attack by a U-boat in the second world war was anything but a proud achievement, the second, which took place on September 16, 1939, off the west coast of Ireland, when Kapitänleutnant Schuhardt sank the aircraft carrier *Courageous,* can be looked on as the first great blow struck by the new submarine branch of the German navy.

But final proof that the U-boats were again, as they had been twenty years before, one of Germany's most telling weapons in the war against Britain was supplied by Kapitänleutnant Prien (then a lieutenant) when in U.47 he succeeded in penetrating the carefully protected main anchorage of the British Fleet in Scapa Flow and sinking the battleship *Royal Oak.*

The same feat had twice been attempted toward the end of the first world war, each of the two U-boats concerned being destroyed. The war diaries of the U-boat Command for September 1939 show that the project had been revived after up-to-date information concerning conditions off Scapa Flow had been obtained by German reconnaissance planes and by the commander of a small U-boat who had been on patrol in the area. From September 8, active preparations for the attempt were being made under the direction of Kommodore Dönitz.

Kirk Sound is one of the lesser of several entrances to Scapa Flow, as it were, a leg of the larger Holm Sound. To the U-boat command its sole protection appeared to consist of blockships sunk athwart the channel at its narrowest places. If navigated with skill and determination, it seemed possible for a small craft to penetrate this passage.

It was decided that the attempt should be made when the period of the new moon, affording complete darkness, coincided with suitable tides for the U-boat to enter and leave

11

the channel. Both these conditions would be fulfilled on the night of October 13-14.

So that it could be refloated in the event of running aground, the U-boat was to attempt to thread its way through the channel into Scapa Flow on the rising tide. If it succeeded, only a short time would be available for attacks on the heavy units which lay at anchor there and then the boat would have to try to find its way out again against the flow of the tide, before the latter reached full strength.

The tidal flow in Pentland Firth, between Scotland and the Orkneys, and in the smaller channels among the islands is enormously strong, reaching at its maximum a speed of anything up to 10 knots, while a U-boat of Type VII had a maximum surface speed of 15-16 knots. When submerged, it was capable of 7 knots for short periods, but normally traveled at 3-4 knots, while, when "creeping" with a minimum of noise, it made an even slower speed. Considerable skill would be required, therefore, to navigate so sluggish a craft as a U-boat through a narrow channel, past two block-ships sunk in its most awkward stretches, on strong tidal waters, varying in speed and direction in accordance with the formation of the banks and the condition of the channel-bed—and all this without giving away its presence to the enemy!

To such a hazardous undertaking Günther Prien was well suited. Of all U-boat commanders then on active service, he had the most thorough sea-going experience, having served in the merchant navy, where he obtained his master's ticket, before transferring to the Kriegsmarine. Moreover, his personal qualities were exactly those most likely to achieve success: a cool head, robust nerves, intelligence and, above all, a zestful and daring spirit.

Instead of being plunged in the darkness of the new moon, however, the night chosen for the raid proved to be brightly lit by the Aurora Borealis. Nevertheless, Prien decided to continue with the attempt. For one thing, the tides were now at their most favorable and if the attack were postponed what guarantee was there he asked himself that the Aurora would be any less brilliant on the following nights? But meanwhile the British fleet might put to sea from Scapa Flow, leaving the anchorage deserted. Finally all preparations were complete and his men tense and ready for action. A postponement would inevitably plunge the crew into a mood of anti-climax

and entail perhaps weeks of planning and renewed preparation before the attempt could be repeated—if, indeed, it
could be made at all.

With violent alterations of its course, Prien steered the
U.47, fully surfaced, through the narrow channel of Kirk
Sound. It was just past low-water and already the tide was
flowing strongly again inshore: the U-boat grazed the second
of the block-ships, but escaped without damage.

Once inside the Flow, Prien crept onward to the southwest, toward the main anchorage. It was empty. That very
day, while the U.47 had been lying on the bottom off Pentland Firth waiting for nightfall, the British fleet had put to
sea.

Behind the boom defenses of the Sound, Prien came upon
British destroyers patrolling the anchorage, and altered course
to search the northern side of the Flow, finding at last two
heavy units anchored close together under the lee of the shore.
From his angle of vision the silhouettes of the hulls over-
lapped, but he was able to identify one as the *Royal Oak*. The
other he took to be the *Repulse*, though it is now known to
have been the obsolescent aircraft carrier, H.M.S. *Pegasus*.

Despite the telltale brilliance of the Northern Lights—in
the waters of the Flow surrounded by the tall black ramparts
of the hills, they seemed to be focused as in a concave mirror
—Prien closed in to short range on the surface and attacked.

Of the entire loading of five torpedoes, only one struck
home, hitting, as it seemed from the U-boat's bridge, the bow
of the second ship projecting from behind that of the *Royal
Oak*.

Surprisingly, after this unmistakable explosion, the expected
reaction from the defense was not forthcoming and for a
while all remained calm. Making away from the target after
firing his last torpedo from the stern, Prien then undertook
the second of that night's hazardous operations. Slowly forg-
ing ahead—not at full speed, as prudence and his prearranged time-table required—he did not make for Kirk
Sound and the safety of the open seas beyond, but stopped in
the middle of the British main fleet anchorage, the scene still
brilliantly illuminated by the Aurora Borealis, to have the
entire spare charge of five torpedoes, now hoisted in readiness,
reloaded into the empty tubes.

Inside twenty minutes—record time, but too long for

Prien, perambulating in the enemy mousetrap with exits now
certain to be doubly guarded—the torpedo-tubes were reported ready for action and he turned again to attack. This
time, fired from the same angle with the same gyro-setting
but at even shorter range, the whole of the salvo struck the
target and, torn by gigantic explosions, the *Royal Oak* was
literally blown into the air.

Now at last the enemy reacted. Holding it to be impossible
for a U-boat to penetrate the anchorage, apparently those responsible for the defense of Scapa Flow had thought the first
torpedo hit was an internal explosion in the *Royal Oak*,
though later they had changed their minds and sounded the
air-raid warning. Meanwhile the U.47 had remained unobserved and unsearched-for.

But now the whole Flow jumped into startled life, search-
lights groped across the water, tracer bullets described their
slow parabolas and the hunt for the rash intruder began in
earnest.

Meanwhile the U.47 turned to make good her escape.
Destroyers appeared from the southeast, one of them bearing down at an acute angle, cutting off the route to Kirk
Sound. The Flow was alive with winking lights as the pursuing
ships signaled to each other. Prien hugged the mainland,
heading to the south of Kirk Sound, so that the U-boat would
merge into the dark background of the surrounding hills. And
still the masthead light of the destroyer was coming closer. . . .

Suddenly, along the coast road, a truck roared up at high
speed, braked sharply and turned, its headlights stroking the
gray hull and conning tower of the submarine. Then the
driver roared off again in the direction from which he came.
Why? Had he seen the dark shape outlined against the silvered
sea? Did he recognize it? What would happen now? Prien
stood racked with uncertainty on the bridge, while the water
swirled and hissed past the boat. Though the Diesel and the
electric motors, coupled together, were both turning at maximum speed she was making only small headway against the
tide racing through the narrow Sound, and the landmarks
dropped all too slowly astern.

And now the destroyer was almost upon her—beneath the
masthead light carried in the harbor area the lean and
hungry-looking silhouette loomed huge against the wan sky
streaked with the Northern Lights. On the bridge the glare of

an Aldis lamp quivered into life. Was he signaling to the others that he had seen the low shape of the U-boat just ahead of him laboring forward against the tide? The lookout men on the bridge blinked involuntarily, awaiting a sudden blinding shaft from the destroyer's searchlight, then the orange-red flame from her guns. . . .

But *has* she seen us, Prien wondered? Apparently not, though the U-boat was making heavy going against the tide, and the propellers, turning at maximum revolutions, left an agonizingly conspicuous band of white, foaming water astern. But if he slackened speed, the boat would be carried back into the Flow.

Slowly the U.47 fought her way forward. It was getting late and the tide was running too strongly now for the engines of a small craft. Has it come to this?" wondered Prien, "the balance-sheet of profit and loss—one battleship as against one submarine? . . . If only that destroyer would alter course one fraction of a point. But he can't miss us now—must see us—must!—

And at that moment the destroyer did alter course and Prien saw her sheer off suddenly to the westward, her mast light wandering away into the gloom. At that same moment the U-boat reached the entry to Kirk Sound. She struggled on, now meeting the full force of the tidal stream in the pent-up waters of the narrow channel, just managed to clear a wooden landing stage projecting into midstream, skirted, with rudder hard over, the two block-ships and at last, still unobserved, reached the open sea.

When Lieutenant Prien returned to base he could look back on an operation carried out with exemplary skill and daring, during which the submarine had not once been attacked. The success which he and the U-boat Command had hoped and aimed for had only partially been achieved and a proportion of the torpedoes fired were defective (we shall return to this later), but that did not detract from the brilliance of his feat nor from the moral prestige which it lent to the new and untried German navy.

The name of Scapa Flow had a special significance for Germans, having been the scene of the scuttling of the German high seas fleet at the end of the first world war, and Prien, as he stated afterward, was thinking of this during the operation that was intended to inflict at one blow and with a single small craft a crippling wound on the British home fleet.

Had the fleet still been in Scapa Flow, there is little doubt that Prien would have succeeded. As late as October 12, the day before the raid, air reconnaissance had shown one aircraft carrier, five heavy units and ten cruisers, besides a large number of smaller vessels, to be present in the Flow. Yet though Prien came too late, he was in time to find a way into the anchorage and if the attempt had been postponed only a few days, it is believed that it would no longer have been possible to force a passage through Kirk Sound.

It appears that some weeks before the operation took place, the British Admiralty, considering the existing defenses inadequate, had decided that a third block-ship should be sunk in Kirk Sound and had earmarked for purchase a suitably aged vessel then lying in the Pool of London. The Treasury at first refused the price asked by the owner of the ship but at last approved on the Admiralty's insistence, only to find additional mooring fees had accrued in the interval. Again the Treasury declined to pay the stipulated sum, again the Admiralty had to supply in full the reasons for its need, until at last the purchase was approved and the Admiralty could take possession of the ship, towing it out of London for its journey to Kirk Sound on October 13, the day on which the fleet had sailed from Scapa Flow and on the night of which Prien had sailed through the channel past the existing defenses. The enemy chivalrously recognized the skill and daring of his feat, which remains unique in the annals of naval warfare.

2 TOUCH AND GO

HERBERT SCHULTZE was one of the first U-boat commanders to make his name and, like Prien, he had been given his first command before the war.

Now his long seagoing experience was to be put to the test. His boat, the U.48, on the trail of two heavily escorted freighters, had maneuvered into position below the horizon, dived to attack and was coming in at periscope depth. Thirty-five minutes after submerging, still unobserved and already through the screen of escorts, he was ready to give the order: "Tube One, fire!" Ten minutes after the explosion the 8,000-

ton British freighter *Navasota* had disappeared. The second
ship escaped, out of range. For a time, Schultze had to hide
as the escort searched for the submerged U-boat, and was
unable to take up the pursuit.

After half an hour, the enemy moved away and he rose to
periscope depth. No sign of life. Surfacing, Schultze was the
first to jump onto the streaming bridge. As always, before
calling up the duty watch, he took a good look around. On
the starboard beam a convoy was coming over the horizon.
He called up the watch, had the convoy's course quickly
worked out and then headed the boat toward the distant blur
of smoke. A few hours, and it would be time to dive in
preparation for attack. Now, to periscope depth and the pursuit. The watch had already gone below again and Schultze
(the commander always being the last to leave the bridge)
was holding on to the upper conning-tower hatch in readiness
to descend. Before doing so, he took a last look, seaward—
all clear: skyward—"DIVE!" A Sunderland—coming straight
for the U-boat. . . .

Schultze scrambled down the hatch, securing the cover
after him, while even before the alarm-klaxon had finished
sounding, the levers in the control room below were pulled
down to open the main vents. The air hissed out and the U-
boat began to dive immediately though far too slowly for the
Commander's liking.

To hasten the process, the leading engineer ordered: "All
hands forward!" and anyone not required to remain at his
action station shoved, slithered and squirmed his way forward,
down the central gangway (still only slightly inclined) through
ward room, E.R.A.s' mess, seamen's mess, head first, almost,
through the second watertight bulkhead down into the torpedo-stowage compartment, through another bulkhead and so
to the fore-ends close by the torpedo tubes.

The depth gauge read barely fifty feet, the superstructure
had only just disappeared beneath the surface, when the boat
was racked and smitten by four heavy explosions—the Sunderland's bombs. Immediately, she slumped steeply down.
Had she been hit, the crew wondered, or was it because of
the extra weight in the bows? But the trim was restored and
no damage was reported.

Then came a new sound, the rapid pulse of a ship's propellers. A destroyer had arrived overhead. Taking her time,

like a hunter certain of the kill, she started to circle slowly, while the U-boat crept on, the sound of the destroyer's Asdic, now loud, now soft, groping round the hull.

The destroyer stopped for a while, felt with her Asdic, then moved on a little to improve her position. Again the propellers paused, again the Asdic's sound waves stroked the hull of the U-boat. Then a few more turns of the propellers and she stopped once more. The sound of the Asdic sawed at their nerves. Then silence—and still silence—finally the depth charges! The first once, directly overhead and with such a roar that the crew involuntarily ducked, while the U-boat shuddered, leaped and pitched like a pendulum, almost out of control. Then the second one—still closer.

Schultze decided to dive deeper, but gently, so that the listeners overhead would hear no more than they must. Then by fractions of a degree he tried to slip away from the course which the enemy had plotted. Twenty minutes after the first series, three more depth charges exploded close by the U-boat, wrecking the angle gauge (essental for depth control), and blowing out the fuses in the telegraph circuit.

The pressure hull withstood the shocks and, as each compartment in turn reported back to the control room "All okay," the crew breathed more freely. It is a terrible feeling to lie blind and motionless beneath the surface waiting for the next explosion, and was especially so in the early days of the war, when no one could predict how much a hull would withstand.

In the comparatively shallow waters of the North Sea, the U-boat had already almost touched the sea-bed. Although the depth was greater than the maximum to which it was considered safe to submerge, Schultze decided to creep down farther and lie on the bottom; the depth charges would do less damage there; at any rate, the U-boat would be out of range of the Asdic and the motors could be switched off and current saved. As far as possible, the auxiliary machinery could be stopped, too, to reduce the telltale noise: the master-gyro with its continual low hum, the fans and the pumps. By this means, perhaps, they might give their pursuers the slip.

But in a few moments, the agonizing sounds began again—the destroyers' propellers, circling, stopping, then the depth charges with their horrible deep roar. How much longer? How long? Washbasins and the toilet were shattered, light bulbs burst; in the conning tower, the revolution-indicator was wrecked.

Must we wait, think the crew, trapped like this, helpless, till the hull splits open under the impact of the explosions and we are swept, choking, to a miserable end? What will the Commander do? We are in his hands. It is up to him. Why doesn't he move, give an order? Is there nothing he can do? Or does he think we are all right as we are, lying here, pinned to the ocean bed?

There was no alternative but to wait, on the chance that with the winter darkness, which in this latitude would fall at about six o'clock, the U-boat could make good her escape on the surface—if, by then, she was able to surface at all. . . .

18.00 HOURS reads the war diary of the U.48, LIFT OFF THE BOTTOM, PROCEED AT 200 FEET. H. E. FADING. . . .

Though the destroyers were still searching overhead, the U-boat managed to slip away unnoticed. For forty-five minutes, she crept dead-slow under the water. Then, with two miles between herself and the enemy, all was quiet above and the pursuit seemed to have been abandoned.

Schultze surfaced cautiously, scrambled up onto the bridge for the first look around and — found he had come up in the middle of a whole group of enemy escort vessels, and he had thought there were only two! It was dark, but a clear night and visibility was good. The seas and the swell were moderating, and the wind had dropped. The low, slim hull of the U-boat lay heaving quietly on the surface and all around the dark shadows of the enemy vessels could be clearly seen.

Schultze counted twenty-four of them. Twenty-four ships hovering over the prey they still believed was lying on the bottom of the sea. Some of them glided softly away and stopped again a little farther off, searching with their Asdic.

So as to make less noise, Schultze had the rudder changed from electric to hand control and continued to engage the motors and not the Diesels. Then, the boat barely moving, he edged the bow toward a gap, the largest he could find, between two of the ships. . . .

"We literally wormed our way out," said the Commander later. DISENGAGED ON THE SURFACE, he reported laconically in the war diary, then, unable to restrain a note of jubilation, added GOT AWAY WITH IT.

I asked him the distance between the two ships. "Oh, about

eight to nine hundred yards, with visibility at the maximum, just as we went through. A bad moment, I can tell you, especially as we were still on edge, after all those depth charges. After a while, we were able to engage the Diesels, but first . . ."

First, a leak had to be repaired in the water-cooling jacket, and elsewhere in the boat the damage was greater than had been reported. The valves on the outer hull were all loose in their seatings, the air vents had been affected, the entire tele-motor system and the gyro and magnetic compasses had been put out of action. There was work enough for every technical rating in the boat, but in a long peacetime training they had learned to deal with such emergencies and the essential equipment was ultimately repaired.

The coxswain made a general issue of Kujambel (juice) and for supper the whole crew had a really good stew, always a favorite in the Kriegsmarine and popularly known as a "half-turn." Nevertheless, morale remained low, each man having so recently looked upon the face of death. Moreover, the crew had not yet acquired that self-confidence and vigorous unconcern which characterized experienced U-boat men and was responsible for their astounding achievements.

During the night, while the U.48 put as many miles as possible between herself and the enemy, the wind and the sea got up and visibility deteriorated. Dawn revealed a bleak and rain-scoured sea, slapping like wet cloths into the faces of the men on the bridge.

Soon an enemy convoy was sighted, but the chief and his Cyclops, as the engine-room ratings were called, were still at work repairing the damage and the boat was not yet cleared for action, much though Schultze would have welcomed an opportunity to restore the morale of his men. He knew exactly how they felt, for it was much the same with him. Their first and prolonged experience of being depth-charged, helpless to do anything but wait passively for what had seemed the inevitable end, had unnerved them and sapped their initiative. For that there was only one remedy—a successful attack.

A short while later, during a sudden rain squall, two destroyers surged past, barely a hundred yards away; the U-boat remained undetected. Soon after, a tanker and another vessel were sighted, apparently stragglers from the previous convoy. Though the boat was by no means yet in fighting trim,

Schultze seized the opportunity and attacked. Number one torpedo was fired, and missed. Number two also missed: too wide a D.A.[1], "And too much by guess and by God," added the Commander later.

Schultze came in for a third attempt. This time, the torpedo struck the heavily laden vessel amidships, tearing her in half. She caught fire and blew up—the British tanker, *San Alberto* of 7,379 tons.

So the depth-charge psychosis was cured; the men had taken their revenge, as they felt, for what was to remain the most gruelling and nerve-racking experience of their U-boat career.

3 THE GALLEY-SLAVE

WE HAVE just sailed for patrol. Five minutes ago the berthing wires were cast off and we stood lined up on the after-casing waving good-by to our friends on the quay: wives, sweethearts, the men from the dockyard who had serviced the boat for patrol and the girls from the staff of the U-boat Hostel at Lorient—they, too, were determined not to miss one last bon voyage.

It is late afternoon now, and as we glide slowly westward toward the harbor mouth the figures on the quay dwindle and merge into the gathering twilight of this cheerless February day; the clash and thump of the military band—*Muss i denn, muss i denn zub Städtele hinaus*—coming ever more faintly to us across the rippling harbor waters, lengthening and falling astern.

As I linger on the open deck, watching the land recede, the stoker (1ST Class) of the off-duty watch comes edging along toward me. He was the first person I saw when I arrived a few hours ago, and when I inquired for the commander, the stoker it was who jumped down and took my suitcase while I negotiated the springy gangplank.

He says now, making his way toward me: "This's the cook; you want to get on good terms with him right away."

I see a broadly beaming face, a shock of hair, cherry-black eyes—a plump, well-cushioned looking youth.

"Oh, we'll get along all right," he says. "Just give a shout

---

[1] Director Angle, *i.e.* aim-off.

when you want any garbage from the galley." And he laughs, in a deep, reverberating bass.

Now others throng round. Someone sees the Leica round my neck: "*Prima*, man! Is it your own?"

"My name's Franz," declares another, then adds—as if he needed to!—"I come from Vienna; and Pepi, here, he's from Styria." Pepi steps forward to shake my hand.

"You see, we've got all sorts here," says the stoker. "The lost German, as we call him, over there, the *Volksdeutsche*, he comes from Poland, partly; Wiellm, here, from Upper Silesia . . ."

And so it goes on, a mass of strange and confusing faces. They look tough, these free-and-easy lads. Most of them have recently shaved, at least as recently as yesterday, but that will soon be changed. Before long, they'll look like real desperadoes.

They're friendly, though, and anxious to help. After all, I am only a guest on board, and a reservist, much older than they.

Now it's almost dark. As the sun was setting, the clouds brooding on the horizon lifted for a moment and a brilliant streak of light quickened along the low coastline by the entrance to the inner harbor, printing on the memory the outline of the ancient church silhouetted on the cliffs above Larmor Plage. Now as we pass the island of Le Groix, lying a few miles off the coast, the escort leaves us to return to harbor and we find ourselves alone on the open sea.

Standing beside the lookouts on the bridge, I can hear the sturdy throb of the Diesels, while coming up through the open hatchway, glowing dully in the faint light from the control room, is that strange, indefinable smell—the U-boat fog, familiar as the breath of home to the old hands among the crew, so familiar that they are hardly aware of it.

In the diminutive galley, the cook is preparing the supper. It has been put back a few hours tonight, because of the late sailing. When the meal is ready, the duty stewards will come staggering along the central gangway to fetch the meal for the seamen in the fore-ends and the petty officers abaft the control room, carrying in one hand the can for the coffee or ready-sweetened tea, and in the other the "long-boat," a deep, bucket-shaped container for the food. As the ship lurches in the seas, they will have an awkward time of it on their return journey, propping themselves against a bulkhead here with their elbows, leaning there, backs pressed against some other support, while the men along their route lend willing hands to see that the supper reaches its destination intact. Those that can't manage a job like this—well, it's just too bad, they're not suited to life in a U-boat and before long they'll be posted ashore.

While the stewards wait at the galley, the mess traps are brought out from the cupboard and the racks—called fiddles —secured to the table to prevent the dishes sliding off with the movement of the boat. In the petty officers' mess, too, a hum of voices has started up in anticipation of the meal.

A hot, grease-smeared face pops out of the galley door and before starting to dish out, the cook issues a preparatory warning, "Fried eggs, three each!" Then he starts counting them out into the containers. After the eggs, come the gherkins, then the steward from the seamen's mess, the "Emissary of the People," goes staggering for'ard again, through the throng in the petty officers' mess, through the circular bulkhead opening, through the control room, through another hoop, past the Commander, who sits reading on his bunk, through the ward room and the warrant officers' mess, and so to the seamen's mess, close to the bows.

For the petty officers, arrangements are more genteel. They have their eggs served straight onto their eating boards, the gherkins are put on a separate plate, the butter in a metal dish, and they are issued thick slices of bacon and sausage, as well. There is tea, with or without lemon juice, and bread is slung in hammocks above the mess tables where everyone can help himself.

Suddenly, in the middle of the meal, comes a shout from the petty officers' mess:

"Music! Hey! Control room! Where's that lazy telegrarfis?" The speaker plants his fists aggressively on the table, knife and fork uppermost. "Here! Control room! Willi! Pass it on, will you? Tell that dope to give us some music! Radio, or records —let him put on some records—only let's have something!"

The message is passed on to the hydrophone operator in his listening booth opposite the Commander's cabin, where the radio and record-player are kept. In a moment or two, from somewhere out of sight in the deckhead, a popular song blares out: "Don't let it get you down!" Halfway through comes the vocal:

> Don't let it get you down!
> Why take life with a frown?
> Bad times will pass,
> And nothing can las',
> So please, sugar, don't let it get you . . .

"Cook!" bawls Erwin. "What's the matter with these eggs? Look at the size of 'em! They're ants' eggs, that's what they are! Go fetch me another half-dozen—no eight'll do. Eight more eggs right here in front of me, or I'll —"

The tone on board is rough and hearty. The men go for each other bull-headed, "horn-mad," as they say.

Now Paul, the navigator (Warrant Officer, 2nd Class), joins in:

"Cook, my eggs tasted of Diesel oil. Did you fry them in Diesel oil? Here, you try them, Herr Funkmaat!" he says, appealing to the P.O. Telegraphist (2nd Class), a quiet, steady man and therefore, it seems to him, a better judge of eggs. "Do you taste anything queer about them? Surely, the oil can't have got through, not right through the shell and all?"

"Yes. Yes, I'm afraid it has," says the expert, assuming a judicial manner, while to make doubly sure, he takes the three eggs from the pan himself and consumes them with an air of grave deliberation. The cook waits anxiously for the verdict, then, none forthcoming, hurries off to fry a few more for Paul, as a concession to his wounded palate.

The men in the seamen's mess usually eat with their bare hands, as Erwin has just been doing, simply lifting the eggs out of the long-boat and stuffing them down, or else eating them without knife or fork on a piece of bread. As to washing their hands afterward—"What?" they'd say. "In the middle of eating your supper? Far too much trouble. Once a day is enough, in that oil-filmed water you get from the tank!"

Meanwhile, the fat is sizzling again in the galley—the last of the eggs. Who's going to eat them? Only Erwin volunteers —astonishing what he can put away, with his small size!

Even when supper is over, the cook still has plenty to do. There is hot water to issue then to each mess for washing up. In the petty officers' mess, they are beginning already to collect the traps, shove the remains of the meal together for the garbage bucket, unrig the fiddles and generally clear up the table, as forlorn-looking now as a battlefield is to a defeated army.

The messman appears with an inch or two of tepid sea water in a bowl, and while he wipes the cutlery, mugs and eating boards, some of the petty officers turn in on their bunks.

The U-boat is far out in the bay now, and rides, long and deep, through the Biscay swell. Above the double tiers of bunks ranged along each side of the hull, the hammocks full of bread swing steadily like slow pendulums to and fro. In three weeks' time, the loaves will be covered with thick, greenish-white mildew—"white rabbits," as the crew call them, when they take them down, holding them vertically, by the "ears." Later, when the loaves have been exhausted, canned bread and crackers will be issued.

At eight bells, 20.00 hours, the men of the outgoing watch will come down for their supper. When they have finished, they will sit around for a while and then turn in. "Hein Seeman"[1] has hardly put his head down when he is asleep, whatever din there may be around him. The radio crackles, whistles and wails at maximum volume with the evening program from Germany: "A Thousand Joyous Notes," it's called. . . .

But the cook's day is not over, even yet. He has no watch-keeping duties, admittedly, and so can sleep through undisturbed at night, but he has to be up early in the morning to get the breakfast.

If the men of the middle watch (12 P.M. to 4 A.M.) want anything during the night, black coffee or eggs, sometimes fried potatoes or omelets, they must make it themselves. Now, before turning in, the cook has one last duty. Armed with keys and a pocket lamp, he goes for'ard to fetch canned food from the store and fresh meat from the ice-chest. In a few moments he returns, balancing cautiously, step by step, along the gangway, with his arms full of tins and filleted veal.

"Tomorrow's dinner," he says, grinning at me, as he goes past.

Dark green curtains, drawn tightly before one of the bunks, suddenly part and a head peers out:

"What you got there? Roofing tiles?"

[1] German equivalent of "Jack Tar."

"Blanquettes de veau," says the chef, in a superior voice, continuing undeterred on his way. "Veal for stewing," he adds, for the benefit of the uneducated.

"Blankets? We've had some queer stews at home, but my mother never give us *blankets to eat.* That ain't the way to treat veal!"

The cook turns and glowers back, wounded in his professional pride. "I don't care what your mother does; *my* mother can make *blanquettes de veau* as well as anybody, and I'll do it her way, if you don't mind. What's more, Mum tips the scales at two hundred and ninety pounds, so she ought to know what's good!"

Stolid, majestic, almost, in his pride, the cook stands there ready for battle, a look of blank, outraged amazement on his face at the roar of laughter that follows; perspiring, slab-cheeked, still twisting a piece of meat in his fingers; with the back of his hand pushing a damp lock out of his eyes, a hero, unsung. . . .

A long pause, then, at last, comes a quieter voice from a bunk: "All right, chum! All right. You're a damn good cook, we all know that. So—good night to you. Good night."

4 THE RED DEVIL BOAT

FEW U-BOAT crews can have functioned better as a team or held together more proudly, despite the fact that the pick were lost to a promotion course after every patrol, than the men of the U.57, one of the small, "coastal" U-boats of 300 tons.

This particular boat bore as an emblem on her conning tower two prancing demons, each bearing aloft a burning torch. They had been put there by her first commander, and it was from them that the U.57 acquired her nickname, the Red Devil Boat. But that was later, when she had become famous. When Erich Topp took over the command, the U.57 was merely the U.57.

On Friday, October 13, 1940, the U.57 was due to set off on patrol, the first under her new commander. Friday the thirteenth! So Erich Topp, mindful of the old superstition, sailed, instead, on the Thursday—sailed right across the harbor to berth again on the opposite side, finished taking on stores and put quietly out to sea on the morrow before Fate had a chance to look around. Or so he hoped.

They were still in the North Sea, a thoroughly murky day, when a drifting mine lurched up, groped and ground its way horribly along the casing, then freed itself and drifted harmlessly away. (According to international agreement, mines that broke loose from their moorings were supposed to unprime themselves automatically, but you never could tell!)

In Norway, Topp replenished his supply of Diesel fuel, then set off to search in earnest for the enemy. Hardly had he left Korsfjord, when, on the silk-smooth sea, one of the lookouts on the bridge spotted the bubble-tracks of two compressed-air torpedoes making straight for the boat. "Hard-a-starboard!" roared the officer of the watch. "Full ahead together!"

Scrambling to the bridge, Topp was just in time to see the tracks go streaking past the boat, a spreading salvo from a British competitor. An attempt to pursue and out-maneuver the enemy submarine failed, owing to a breakdown in the hydrophone gear, and the U.57 was forced to disengage.

The first part of the patrol lasted for five days, and within that time the small number of torpedoes which the coastal-type U-boat could accommodate had all been expended. Topp had sunk a lone steamer bound for Britain with a cargo of timber, and another ship traveling in convoy and loaded with ammunition. Despite the continued strike of the hydrophones, he had evaded the subsequent rain of depth charges from the escorting destroyers and earned a congratulatory signal from Dönitz: *Well done, U-57! Keep it up!*

A quick call at Bergen to replenish supplies and the U.57 again put to sea. In foggy weather off the northwest coast of Scotland, a gigantic convoy was sighted, but at the decisive moment the new engineer officer failed to put on the trim and Topp had to let the convoy go; it was the biggest he was ever to set eyes on during the whole of his career at sea.

In the North Channel, at the entrance to the Irish Sea, the U.57 came upon a 5,000-tonner, sinking her after an arduous pursuit and at the fourth attempt. Then, spotted too late for the U-boat to submerge, a plane dropped bombs, fortunately all duds.

Next, Topp put into Lorient, again to replenish supplies. On the way north the boat was again attacked by aircraft, holed fifteen times by machine-gun fire, but nobody hurt. The plane dropped one bomb, which failed to explode.

In barely a week, the boat was again in the North Channel,

and for ten days the little ship battled through heavy seas
amid unrelenting storm. For ten days, no sight or sound but
the lash and splutter of the spray, the sky's lament, and the
wind's despair. The hydrophones had been temporarily repaired, but on the very first day of the storm they broke down
again, depriving the Commander of his only contact with the
outside world when the U-boat was submerged.

Eleventh day out of Lorient—sea moderated to Force 6—
steamer in sight and coming closer. The boat bounds about
like a tennis ball. She simply cannot be held at periscope
depth for a daylight underwater attack, slicing down, lifting
again, the bow, even the conning tower, breaking surface, then
slumping once more into the trough of the waves, till finally
she finds herself following close in the wake of the escaping
enemy. His name is just discernible on the stern: *Ceramic*.
But in such seas pursuit is impossible. He's lucky. Sixteen
thousand tons—what a haul! Already, in the first world
war, the *Ceramic* had survived three separate U-boat attacks;
some ships are like that.

Thirteenth day. With daylight a plane comes diving suddenly out of low cloud. This time the bombs are distinctly
unpleasant and the boat is badly shaken. One of the Diesels
is ripped off its bed, the camshaft snaps and most of the instruments are smashed. The boat dives—luckily the pressure-
hull is still watertight—and being close to the land and in
shallow water, she can be laid on the bottom.

While the damage is being repaired, the Commander dis-
cusses the situation with his officers. The chief engineer, as
the man responsible for the technical functioning of the boat,
urges emphatically that they should return to base. Diesels are
beyond repair and the rest of the damage can at best only be
patched up in the hope that somehow they will manage to
struggle home. Reichenbach, the young officer of the watch,
suggests, on the other hand, that they cannot possibly return
home without firing a single torpedo, the whole set untouched
and intact.

The Commander agrees. But how can they get within range
of a target with a crippled boat, maximum surface speed, 9
knots? The only chance would seem to be to station themselves at some point which the enemy more or less *has* to pass
and wait there until something happens. Only the chief objects. Resolved: return to North Channel.

So at nightfall, the U.57 goes pounding laboriously back into the narrows, passing several destroyers unobserved. On shore, the navigational beacons are still burning. In the first world war the Irish Sea had been one of the U-boats' principal hunting grounds, but today, with their carefully thought-up system of air and sea patrols, with their anti-U-boat defense operating with such smooth efficiency, the British believe they can afford to let their lights burn on. U-boats? So far inside home waters? Impossible! Thanks to the beacons, the U.57 can be navigated with marvelous precision.

Cautiously, Topp worms his way on the surface deeper and deeper into the lion's den, still unobserved, past all the enemy patrols. How long can this last, he wonders?

A few hours after entering the narrows, he sights an approaching convoy. Fortunately, the moon is hidden. With grim perseverance, Topp maneuvers into position and as he runs out, fires the whole salvo of three torpedoes. Soon after the first has left the tube, the U-boat is sighted by a destroyer on the starboard flank of the convoy. To fire his second shot Topp has to head straight toward a second destroyer, stationed between the lines of ships. The track gives him away, and immediately both destroyers turn and make toward him at high speed.

Meanwhile, the first torpedo strikes its target with a heavy explosion, then the second. But before Topp can have his third shot, there is still some way to go. At last the sights come on and he hears the officers of the watch: *"Rohr drei— Llosss!"* feels the boat falter as the third torpedo leaves its tube, then: "Control room, control room! DIVE—DIVE— DIVE!" The main vents are opened, while on the bridge the night-sight is unrigged at top speed and vanishes through the hatch with the lookouts. Last to leave, the Commander scrambles down, clamping the cover behind him.

Now, as the boat is diving (in only 25 fathoms), the third explosion is heard, again, a direct hit. Suddenly, a broad stream of water curves into the bow compartment and, seconds later, the nose of the boat bumps heavily on the bottom. Hell!

"Blow for'ard!" Quick! Away from the diving position before the destroyers are on us! Off the bottom, come on, up! What's happened? Changeover valve still open! Now, as the bow lifts, the stern immediately slumps to the bottom and sticks there. Too much water in the boat, three tons in excess of her diving weight.

The roar of the depth charges begins.

"Belay bilge pumps!" All machinery is stopped so as not to give away the position to the enemy sound detectors and the boat lies quietly on the bottom. Meanwhile the seawater that has broken in is collected, bucketful by bucketful, and dispersed evenly throughout the bilges. In this way perhaps the trim can be restored.

And still the depth charges go on erupting, all around the boat, far too close for comfort. The damage mounts. After every explosion, new leaks in the hull are reported, spurts and drips of water are everywhere.

Now the lights go out and in the darkness animal fear grows, feeding on uncertainty. Topp forces himself to speak in an easy, conversational tone, asks a question, makes some light remark, shielding the men from the truth, for the truth is that their fate stands poised upon the razor's edge. . . .

The depth-charging goes on for the rest of that night, and the following day, and yet another night. Every half-hour one of the pursuers glides past overhead, unloading as he goes.

Then, each time, there is a pause—the minutes tick by— no sound—and still no sound—can it be? Here they come again, the destroyer's propellers. Oh, God they're stopping; the Asdic's pinpointing the boat—they're starting again—look out, here it comes. . . .

A cavernous roar, then another, till it seems incredible that the boat can still survive. Perhaps she is lying in a fold of the seabed, sheltered from the full impact of the blast, is that the explanation?

Another hour passes. The air is foul, the air-conditioning plant no longer functioning. Topp sends the crew to their bunks. Each man is given a potash cartridge with a tube on the end to breathe through. He puts the tube in his mouth, and as he breathes through it, the potash removes the carbon dioxide. The Commander and the officer of the watch sit huddled on the chart cupboard in the control room, the only place they can find, for normally the whole crew are never off duty at the same time and bunks are provided for only half the complement.

The remainder lie huddled in their blankets on the bare steel plates of the deck, some of them in inches of water, and the

Commander has to pick his way carefully over them as he goes the rounds every half-hour with a flashlight to make sure that the tubes have not slipped out of the mouths of those who are sleeping.

Yes, some of these youngsters are actually asleep, free as they are of responsibility, free of the necessary imaginative power to foresee — and foretaste — the end. Toward midday, they begin to feel hungry. No hot food can be prepared, so sandwiches are made and passed round. They eat them lying down.

Meanwhile, the air in the U-boat is getting more and more oppressive, can be breathed only in quick, shallow gasps. All around, the explosions continue. Then again there is a pause, till propellers can be heard revolving very slowly, directly overhead. Suddenly, there is a jerk, the bow is lifted up, falls back again. The men jump, wild-eyed, to their feet, then freeze, motionless, listening. . . .

There! Hear it? Something scratching along the hull. "Sweep-wires!" whispers the second officer. The Commander nods, thinks: Must keep calm, the flick of an eyelash, and there'll be panic —

The wires scour over the casing, then fall away astern. The sound of the propellers grows softer as the destroyer drags for the U-boat farther off. Every now and then a depth charge is dropped. The hull rocks and creaks, dribbling everywhere. The last bilge pump goes out of action. If the fuel bunkers were not contained inside the pressure-hull in this type of boat, some Diesel oil would long ago have risen to the surface, marking the spot for the kill.

The hours creep on, the darkness within the boat spreading to the world outside. Here in the hull night has long since fallen, suffocating, clammy, the stagnant horror of the tomb. . . .

The pursuers draw away and once more silence returns. This time, after more than two hundred depth charges, they seem satisfied that their work is done.

22:30 All quiet, manage to get bilge pump working. Hope to surface at 23.00.

22.40 Still quiet.

22.50 More depth charges. Will have to wait now till midnight, at least.

14.00 Blow all tanks. Rise off the bottom.

The U-boat surfaces, the conning-tower hatch flies open and sharp, clean air pours into starved lungs. Sea Force 6, pitch-black night: couldn't be better. One destroyer, one other vessel stopped and just discernible dead astern, but lying so low in the water the submarine is harder for them to see and they do not stir. "Group down, slow ahead together." Almost noiseless at this speed the electric motors are engaged instead of the Diesel and the U-boat creeps off on the surface, her presence still undetected.

Both compasses are out of action and there is not a star in the sky. No chance of a navigational fix. But the storm is still blowing, probably from the northwest, as it was forty-eight hours ago when last observed. It means taking a chance, but as the only hope of escaping from the death-trap of the North Channel, Topp sets a course head-on into the seas.

Meanwhile every available man gets feverishly to work repairing the internal damage. By daylight the magnetic compass is clear again and Topp can verify his position. He finds that his guess was right and that now, at last, the U.57 is upon the open seas.

The boat dives so that the two torpedoes remaining in reserve can be loaded into the tubes, then surfaces again. Aircraft on the starboard bow! And in the distance, smoke clouds —a convoy. Down quickly, then full speed toward it, just in time to catch a lone ship straggling at the tail. Topp runs out to attack, firing two torpedoes. The tanker explodes in a ball of fire, dense clouds of pitchy smoke surging upward and spreading to the farthest corners of the sea.

A special U-boat chaser pursues them, dropping depth charges, eighty of them, with twice the explosive power of the earlier ones. The boat rattles and shakes, suffering yet further damage. But this time she can descend to a greater depth and, though slowly, continue to move, making good her escape.

At last the hunt is broken off and all is quiet again. Now Topp can lay his brave boat on the ocean bed, allow his crew and himself to rest, wonderfully peaceful at last, and undisturbed.

A monster gala banquet is prepared (to become traditional in the Red Devil Boat, after the last fish has been fired and the bow has turned toward home). All the delicacies that the kitchen and cellar can produce—and the U-boats didn't do badly for food—are brought out to be recklessly consumed. A bill of fare is passed around so that, informally and according to rank, as the official phrase would have it, each member of the crew can mark off the items of his choice.

Then the great meal is served, Topp sitting with his men, now no longer the new commander on his first patrol, but the Old Man, the man to be trusted, the man who now sits, numb with exhaustion, after leading them through mortal perils to the performance of memorable deeds.

But the U.57, the boat that sailed on Friday the thirteenth, was not yet at the end of her voyage.

On the following day, the one Diesel still in action developed clutch trouble. The reversing clutch was adapted for forward drive and the boat went hobbling on. Each day she was attacked several times by aircraft, each time diving to avoid the bombs and bullets. At last, despite the vigilance of the lookouts, an enemy plane was sighted too late and a hail of bullets descended on the boat as she was submerging to safety. She was holed in ten places, but no one was injured.

So she continued homeward, till one evening just after nightfall she drew in toward Brunsbüttel. Signal contact was established with the movement staff at the lock on the seaward side of the canal and the all clear was given to come in. The lock gates opened. A Norwegian steamer began to move out as the U-boat started to move in. "Red-to-Red!" Then suddenly the steamer's green light was visible, too. With his stern still inside the lock in slack water and his bow just through the gates in a tide running at four knots, the Norwegian was carried, helpless, across the bows of the U-boat. "Full astern!" roared Topp—too late.

There was a grinding shock as the U-boat was rammed. A split-second's frozen horror, then Topp ordered all hands overboard. The conning tower swung wildly, brushing the side of the steamer at deck-level, then the boat went down. In fifteen seconds, she had disappeared.

In that short time, the majority of the men managed to scramble overboard, to be seized immediately by the fast-flowing tide and carried out to sea. After an all-night search, the survivors were finally brought together.

One of them had been in the W/T office when the boat went down. When she came to rest on the bottom, he had found himself standing, with his head in an air bubble. Several times he tried to find his way, swimming underwater, to the conning-tower hatch in the adjacent compartment, returning after each attempt to the air-bubble to regain his breath. At the eighth attempt, he succeeded, only to find the hatch blocked by the bodies of his messmates, drowned while trying to open it. He clawed them aside, groped for the hatch cover, forced it open and so came to the surface. He was found that night, unconscious and totally exhausted, having been washed ashore by the tide.

With the gray December daylight, he insisted on joining his comrades of the U.57 to report to the Commander. Just as they were, some still huddled in blankets, they strung out, a sad, exhausted group. The senior took a pace forward, then spoke, slowly, his voice reduced to a whisper from the salt water that had scored his throat: "Herr Oberleutnant. Crew present, sir, all but six. I've been asked—to ask you, sir—we'd all like to put in to stay together as a crew, sir—and may we have you, sir, please, as our commander—"

It seemed as if Topp were about to speak, but no sound came from his lips. Like most of his crew, he was bareheaded, so he could not salute. They saw him stand there motionless, for a moment, in the icy wind, then turn and walk slowly away.

PART II

SUMMER 1940 — SPRING 1942

The Battle Reviewed

U-BOAT BASES ON THE ATLANTIC

DURING THE second half of 1940, the factors affecting U-boat operations were, on balance, highly favorable.

Before the fall of France and the occupation of the French Atlantic ports, the U-boats had been confined to bases in the North Sea—where the shallow depth enabled the enemy to mine the shipping lanes and virtually dominate the narrow channel between Scotland and Norway.

With the occupation of Lorient, St. Nazaire, Brest, La Pallice and Bordeaux, U-boats could operate from bases much closer to Britain's main sea arteries and much more difficult for the enemy to block with mines on account of their proximity to deep water.

At these ports, starting with Lorient, work was begun at once on the construction of massive U-boat shelters, intended to be bombproof and so well fulfilling the intention that, after the concrete had been further thickened, not even the largest bombs employed toward the end of the war, nor the linked bombs that exploded successively on the same spot, were able to break them open.

Moreover, under the guidance of German technicians, the foreign workers at these ports became increasingly skillful, until finally the dockyard services were no less efficient than those in Germany. In the winter of 1940, the number of U-boats at sea touched the lowest figure of the war, but from the following spring, thanks to these and other measures, new construction remained in excess of losses and an ever-increasing number of flotillas could be brought into being.

THE THREATENED INVASION OF BRITAIN

By the summer of 1940, as the British gained in experience, their anti-U-boat measures were becoming increasingly effective. This advantage was more than outweighed, however, by the necessity which faced them of taking destroyers off convoy duty in order to hold them in the English Channel in readiness for the threatened invasion.

As a result, convoys were only poorly protected during this period and the U-boats were able to achieve some astonishing successes. Attacking in groups at night on the surface, they fought a series of brief but large-scale battles in which whole convoys were almost totally destroyed. During October, 1940, for example, out of one convoy alone, 173,000 gross tons (31 ships) were sunk in one night; on the following night, 110,000 gross tons (17 ships); and, in the days that followed, a further 43,000 tons of the scattered ships that remained.[1]

That was the time when each boat would return home from patrol to report the sinking of forty or fifty thousand tons of shipping, the heyday of the Ace commanders, Prien, Kretschmer, Schepke, Frauenheim, Kuhnke, Schultze and Endrass.

THE GROWING POWER OF DEFENSE

But in September, 1940, the United States transferred fifty destroyers to Britain where they were at once pressed into service, and, as winter approached and invasion became daily more improbable, the British destroyers as well began to return to convoy duty. Thus the conditions which had been so favorable to the U-boats in the preceding months were brought to an end.

In the following year, while special convoy escort groups were being set up and trained, new U-chasers appeared of a type suitable for mass-production, among them the corvette, a vessel smaller than the destroyer, but with improved depth-charge throwers and multiple pompoms. In the air also, anti-U-boat patrols were gathering in strength and scope. Seaborne aircraft were now carried in the convoys themselves, both by

[1] These figures exceed by nearly 25,000 tons the total of British shipping losses for the whole month of October 1940.—*Translator*.

the new escort carriers (which first appeared in September, 1941) and, singly, by some of the merchant ships.

Finally, the enemy was becoming more skillful in evading the night attacks of surface U-boats. Aided by parachute flares and star-shells, the ships could now rarely be persuaded to scatter in confusion, as they had done a few months before. Now the merchant captains performed faithfully their allotted part, cooperating, each time with greater precision, with their naval escorts according to a prearranged plan. There was no panic; many of them had lost ship after ship, yet still they went on sailing, while of their shipwrecked crews, a very high proportion always managed, often in adventurous circumstances, to reach Britain again to rejoin that seafaring band upon whom her survival depended.

A New Generation of U-boat Commanders

Thus, in their attacks on convoys, the U-boats fought on increasingly less favorable terms, and of those more successful commanders who remained at sea, some seemed to find difficulty in adapting themselves with sufficient speed and thoroughness to the change. Despite the astounding improvements in the skill and endurance of crews, the manner in which U-boats were handled fell gradually away from that standard of ruthless daring which it was folly to exceed but essential to attain if any kind of success was to be achieved.

By September, 1941, most of the older generation, the men who had been in command of U-boats since before the war, were either dead or otherwise lost to seagoing service. Some had been posted to training duties ashore, others promoted to command the newly formed U-boat flotillas or to take up appointments on Admiral Dönitz' staff. The three outstanding commanders, Prien, Schepke and Kretschmer, had been lost within the space of a few days in March, 1941. Prien's boat, the U.47, was destroyed with all hands while attacking a convoy on March 8 by the British destroyer, *Wolverine*. Kretschmer, at that time Champion Shot with the destruction of 300,-000 tons to his credit, was picked up and taken prisoner by a British destroyer during a convoy battle on March 17, after he and some of his crew had succeeded in escaping from the sinking U.99. In the same battle, Schepke lost his life in the U.100.

Of the generation who succeeded these veterans, some had sailed as their predecessors' first lieutenants, for example, Endrass with Prien in the U.47 and Suhren with Schultze in the U.48. Others were entirely new to the U-boat Service.

THE EXTENSION OF U-BOAT OPERATIONS

South and Mid-Atlantic

With the Allied occupation of Iceland and the Azores in 1941 and their subsequent development as air bases, Allied air patrols could cover a much wider area, and the U-boats were forced to operate farther out toward the South and Mid-Atlantic, where the vast ocean spaces favored the defense rather than the attack. In these areas, it was principally the larger, Type IX U-boats of 740 tons from the Second Flotilla at Lorient which were employed.

The Mediterranean

In November, 1941, the U-boats made their first appearance in the Mediterranean. The Italians were proving unable to protect the sea routes supplying Rommel and the Africa Corps and were having no more success in attacking the British communications. It was arranged for a flotilla of German U-boats to go to their assistance. In return, an Italian submarine flotilla was sent to Bordeaux for operations in the Atlantic. In due course, 24 out of 35 German U-boats succeeded in penetrating the Straits of Gibraltar and reaching Italy. The submarine base at La Spezia was put at their disposal and a portion of the naval dockyard there. Later, they were based, as well, on Pola, Salamis (Greece) and Toulon.

In the narrow, landlocked Mediterranean, with its clear water and frequently calm seas, the operations of the U-boats proved peculiarly difficult and costly, particularly as they encountered strong enemy air activity, against which they had at first to defend themselves with an antiaircraft armament reinforced only by Italian Bredas, mounted in watertight boxes on the bridge.

The Arctic

Finally, with the invasion of Russia, U-boat operations were still further extended. The boats of the Arctic flotilla set out from their bases in northern Norway to assault the British and later the British-American convoys sailing to Murmansk and Archangel. In this area, their difficulties were increased by the perpetual day which prevailed in summer and the perpetual night in winter.

THE NETWORK OF U-BOAT COMMUNICATIONS

A separate U-boat command was in due course set up for both the Mediterranean and the Arctic areas, but during this period of the war the center of all U-boat operations was in Kerneval, at the mouth of the inner harbor at Lorient, opposite the fortress town of Port Louis. Here Dönitz, the Admiral of U-boats, had his modest headquarters, with Captain, later Rear-Admiral Godt, as chief of the operations staff and throughout the war his closest adviser. The headquarters were moved later to Angers, 150 miles southwest of Paris, thereafter to Berlin, then, in 1944, to Lager Koralle, not far from Bernau, and finally to Flensburg, on the German-Danish border.

Throughout the world, wherever they were operating, the U-boats were in wireless communication with these headquarters, as were the separate area headquarters. By this means it was possible for the reports of all patrolling U-boats to be centrally assessed and for operational plans to be worked out and issued in the form of orders.

WOLF-PACK TACTICS

By June, 1941, the number of U-boats at sea had risen to thirty-two, and Admiral Dönitz was then able to introduce his so-called wolf-pack tactics.

As soon as information of a convoy was received at his headquarters, the U-boats nearest to its reported position were ordered to carry out reconnaissance patrols on courses which the convoy might be expected to cross. If contact was made, the U-boat concerned would immediately report the convoy's position, speed and course, together with the time at which it was first sighted, so that the other U-boats in the vicinity insofar as they had not already acted on their own initiative when they listened in to the contact report, could close in to attack the convoy.

At first, they did this independently, but later it became the

practice for permission to attack to be withheld by headquarters until the whole pack had assembled, thus insuring
that contact was not lost with the convoy and that the attack,
when it came, would be the more formidable for being con-
certed.

Having once scented danger, the convoys would of course
do all they could to deceive and shake off their pursuers and
to defeat this the U-boats would be in constant touch, both
among themselves and with headquarters, the signals to each
being read by all. Though he was unable to decipher the complicated code used in normal transmissions, the enemy could
locate their source and often in this way he obtained warning
of approaching U-boats in time to evade them. At first his
R.D.F. did not register on short wave, and this was accordingly used by U-boats for purposes of intercommunication.
Otherwise, when closing with a convoy, they observed wireless silence.

The contacting of British convoys was simplified during
this period of the war by the fact that they used a fairly
straightforward signaling code which headquarters was able
to decipher, passing the information thus obtained to the wolf
packs. German Naval Intelligence rendered further assistance,
and finally the U-boats themselves increased their range of
visual spotting, at first by seating a lookout in a bosun's chair
mounted at the top of the extended periscope and later by
means of the Bachstelze, a one-man observation kite which
was trailed by the surface submarine.

THE AMERICAN SHOOTING SEASON[1]

To this phase of the U-boat war belongs the so-called
American Shooting Season, that period of phenomenal sinkings off the western Atlantic seaboard that followed the opening of hostilities between Germany and the United States.
They coincided with a general falling-off in the U-boats' success, owing to a multiplication of the difficulties under which
they were operating. It is necessary to say a few words on the
events that led up to the German-American war.

The American Neutrality Act, passed before the outbreak

[1] This chapter is not historically accurate except in one sense—it
represents an average German attitude to the events described.—
Translator.

of the second world war, stipulated that in the event of an armed conflict in Europe an embargo was to be placed on the export of war materials and the granting of credit facilities to the belligerent countries. Goods not included under war materials had, under the Cash-and-Carry Clause of the Act, to be paid for in cash and fetched from the United States by the purchaser. President Roosevelt, having once before attempted to obtain the repeal of the arms embargo, now succeeded in persuading Congress to renew the Cash-and-Carry Clause which had lapsed in the spring of 1939, and in such a way that instead of being a corollary to the arms embargo, as originally intended, it was now interpreted as replacing it.

At that time only the Allies were able to avail themselves of the opportunity which Cash-and-Carry offered, which doubtless accorded with Roosevelt's intention when he obtained its renewal.

But that was not by any means his only departure from strict neutrality. From the very first days of the war, American naval forces had been assisting the British war effort arbitrarily, without the approval of Congress and in a manner entirely repugnant to international law. They kept careful check on the German merchant ships, which, finding themselves at the outbreak of war in American harbors, were attempting to return home through the British blockade. The American ships never let them out of their sight and, under the pretense of escorting them, reported periodically in clear their own and hence the German's position to the American shore stations—in other words to the British Admiralty. As a result, British forces were able without difficulty to locate and intercept the German ships, whose only recourse was to scuttle themselves.

In September, 1940, there followed the transfer of the fifty destroyers to Britain, a yet more flagrant infringement by the American government of its own Neutrality Act, as well as of the Hague Convention. The United States obtained in return the 99-year lease of the Bermuda Islands. At this time the British naval forces alone were totally inadequate to safeguard the sea supplies of food and war materials required to sustain the war effort of the Island People; how the situation would have developed if the American destroyers had not been forthcoming is problematical indeed.

President Roosevelt did not rest content with this "help in

need" for one of the belligerents. Before many months were out, Cash-and-Carry was, in its turn, abandoned as imposing unacceptable restrictions on the scope of his aid for England and he announced to Congress that the most immediate and constructive contribution which the United States could make toward the welfare of humanity was to serve as arsenal for the nations who were at war with "aggressor states." "The stage will soon be reached," he stated, "when they can no longer pay cash for these things" (by that was meant the many billions of dollars' worth of arms which he himself had hitherto been exporting). "But we cannot," he continued, "and we will not tell them that they must capitulate for the sole reason that they are not temporarily in a position to pay for the weapons which they now urgently require."

From April, 1941, United States naval and air forces were openly assisting Britain in the war at sea, shadowing Axis vessels and broadcasting their position in uncoded signals. Meanwhile, the latter, among them the "auxiliary cruisers" or commerce raiders, were still not permitted to retaliate.

For the time being, America refrained from direct hostilities, but Secretary of State Hull declared: "Ways and means must be found of insuring that the aid which we send to Britain reaches its destination in the largest possible quantities and in the shortest possible time." Colonel Knox, the Naval Secretary, was more precise: "We cannot afford to stand by and watch our consignments sunk on the way over. If we do, we shall be defeated, for this battle is our own battle."

The next step toward open war was the American occupation in July, 1941, of Danish Iceland, lying on the flank of the convoys sailing between Britain and America. At the same time, United States forces took over the protection of British convoys for that part of their route which lay between America and Iceland and, two months later, in the whole of the western half of the Atlantic.

Though America was still officially neutral, the activities of her armed forces were indistinguishable from those of a declared enemy of the Axis. Nevertheless, American propaganda continued to dwell on the theme of neutrality and, indeed, what hurry was there, from her point of view, to acquire the official status of a belligerent? The American people were content, for all they saw of the war was a drop in the unemployment figures, and meanwhile America was reaping excellent profits at negligible risk and, at the same time as she was helping Britain to subjugate Germany, turning her British industrial competitor into a dependent.

Germany, for her part, took care to avoid any action that might be interpreted by Japan as provoking the United States to war, for in that case, Japan might consider herself released from her obligations under the Tripartite Pact.[1]

The situation that existed in the summer of 1941 was bound to lead to incidents, for though German U-boat commanders had strict orders not to attack American warships, in behavior and appearance the latter were so similar to the British that it was often impossible to distinguish between them. They were cooperating closely now with the Royal Navy in protecting the British convoys and if U-boats were encountered they did not hesitate to attack them, while their identification was complicated by the fact that fifty destroyers designed and built in America were now sailing under the British Ensign.

Thus, on September 4, 1941, the U.652 was pursued and depth-charged by a destroyer. The German commander succeeded in firing two torpedoes, both of which missed their target. Not until the following day did he learn that his assailant had been the U.S.S. *Greer*.

Immediately, a clamorous outcry arose in the American press and radio, with much show of moral indignation that a "German pirate" had dared to fall upon a neutral vessel. In fact, the incident provided Roosevelt with a long-awaited opportunity, and in a broadcast on September 11, after announcing that a German U-boat had made a premeditated attack on a United States destroyer—(engaged, as his listeners would assume, on her lawful occasions)—he went on to issue the famous "Shoot first" order, saying with pathos: "United States naval and air forces will no longer be called upon to wait until the U-boats lurking beneath the seas have already carried out their murderous intent. . . ."

On September 15, 1941, Colonel Knox announced that the U.S. Navy had been ordered "to seek out and destroy any raider that attempts to interfere with ocean traffic, whether surface vessel or submarine."

In the following month, the U.S. destroyer *Kearney* was

---

[1] Concluded in September 1940 between Germany, Italy and Japan and obliging Japan to support the Axis in Europe if America went to war on behalf of Britain.—*Translator*.

torpedoed and damaged by a German U-boat and another U-boat sank the destroyer *Reuben James*.

Finally, on November 13, by a majority of eighteen, the House of Representatives approved legislation initiated by the President to repeal the provisions under those parts of the neutrality laws still in force which forbade the defensive arming of American merchant ships and the entry of American ships or citizens into the zone of hostilities.

Thus Roosevelt and his circle had gained their ends and, though still not officially at war, for all practical purposes the United States was now the declared enemy of the Axis Powers.

To reach the convoys, U-boats would now have to attack American as well as British warships and the question therefore arose whether it would be preferable to abandon the U-boat campaign altogether, rather than continue it at the price of open war with America.

Germany was still cogitating these grim alternatives, when on December 7, 1941, Japan attacked the American fleet at Pearl Harbor. The dilemma was now resolved, and there followed a declaration of war by Germany on the United States, enabling the Kriegsmarine to strike back at last at the enemy who had long since been fighting under the guise of neutrality.

Nevertheless, the American defense was completely unprepared for the appearance of U-boats on the West Atlantic seaboard, largely, no doubt because their range had been underestimated. At first in North American coastal waters and then progressively farther south toward the Caribbean, the U-boats found conditions infinitely more favorable to success than those encountered on the North Atlantic convoy routes.

Here there were no difficulties in making and maintaining contact, no powerful and well-trained escorts. Most of the ships encountered were sailing singly, and where they were escorted the destroyers were not fitted with Asdics. And they were not handled with the same skill and determination as the British destroyers.

Operating off open anchorages and undefended harbors, the U-boats enjoyed for a time a veritable Eldorado and their sinkings rose to undreamed-of figures—in six and a half months, over 2,500,000 tons. Targets were so plentiful that it was more often lack of torpedoes than shortage of fuel which compelled the U-boats to turn for home.

But the U-boat Paradise, as the British called it, was not destined to be eternal, and when the Americans developed, in their turn, an effective defense, the U-boats had once again to move, this time yet farther afield, where the chances of success diminished as the distance from their base increased.

Meanwhile, though the total number of U-boats in service continued to grow, the spring of 1942 was to mark the turning point in their tide of success, for thereafter, even though the peak sinkings of the whole war were achieved in November, 1942, the tonnage sunk per U-boat began to decline.

Fighting Patrols

5 THE SHIP THAT SAILED ALONE

WHEN THE U-boat came to the surface, the sky to the northwest was one solid wall of cloud. The boat writhed and twisted in the mounting seas and soon, as she began to take it green over the bridge, the lookouts were cramming on oilskins and sou'westers. The Commander clambered down the conning tower and went below, happy that at last he could sleep long and undisturbed.

But the thoughts continued wheeling in his mind. The strain of the last few days had left him exhausted and on edge, and the violent movement of the boat made it impossible to relax.

Like some demented rocking-horse, the U.93 plunges on into the rising storm. Beside the Commander's bunk his leather jacket and binoculars hang ready to hand from a hook on the side of the locker. Each time the boat rolls (or the steamer, as the crew prefer to call her), they swing out into the passageway, then pause, curiously stiff and slanting, in mid-air.

Kapitänleutnant Korth watches them dazedly for a moment, then draws the heavy green curtain which shuts off his bunk and writing-flap from the rest of his "cabin" and affords an illusion of privacy. Wedging himself more securely in his bunk, right knee and elbow pressing against the padded wall on the inside, bottom and left foot against the safety board on the outside and the bolster stuffed behind his back, he turns his face to the wall and closes his eyes.

Hardly has he done so when the men of the relieving watch come staggering and squelching past on their way to the bridge. Then, from the opposite direction, come the men of the outgoing watch, the lookouts from the bridge and the engine-room ratings. One after the other, they swing themselves with smooth, familiar movements through the circular bulkhead opening and disappear, chattering and trampling, towards the bow.

Close by, out of sight beyond the green curtain, the last officer of the watch is peeling off his oilskins. Korth hears the heavy gumboots crash against the locker as he shakes them off, then a sudden creak as he flings himself onto his bunk, then the jangle of the curtain rings, then silence. . . .

Now there are no sounds but the familiar ones; the surge of the water over the casing, the thump and shiver of the waves as they strike up against the conning tower, and from inside the boat, the drawn-out creak of some wooden frame-member each time she rolls, a sudden whir as somewhere a bilge pump springs to life, and from the engine room, the rhythmic hammering of metal against metal.

To Korth, these are the sounds of home and of uneventful routine and slowly, after the convoy battle of the last few days, they lull him to sleep.

Night comes, bringing no slackening of the storm. With the dawn, its fury is still unabated. It rages throughout the day with no sign of easing and on into the second night. Then suddenly it is spent. The wind drops to a sigh, but a strong swell continues, building up the seas into massive wave-mountains.

In the early dawn the boat is dived for trimming and checking of fuel supplies. As always underwater, when the engines no longer interfere with the hydrophones, the operator is at his station in the listening room, a cupboard-like space opposite the Commander's cabin. He adjusts the headphones and listens, frowning with concentration.

"H.E.[1] bearing Green O-eight-five—propeller noises!"

Korth drops his book, holds the headphones to his ear.

"Yes, propellers all right, long way away, though. Not a destroyer, definitely; might be a freighter? Well done!" He nods encouragingly to the lad who is playing the wheel round the bearing.

[1] Hydrophone Effect.

"Chief, periscope-depth," calls the Commander in the direction of the circular bulkhead opening that leads to the control room. "Got your trim worked out yet?" Then, turning to the boy at the hydrophones: "Don't lose those noises; keep singing out the bearings."

He slips into his leather coat, ducks his head through the strap of the binoculars, fastens the sou'wester carefully under his chin (now, while there's time) and waits in the control room till the chief has finished working out the trim and he can go to periscope depth.

"H.E. Bearing Green O-seven-two," comes in a throaty voice from the P.O. telegraphist who has meanwhile taken over the hydrophones. "H.E. Bearing O-seven-two," repeats the control-room messenger, through the door in the bulkhead.

"Thank you."

Having put on the trim, the chief crouches on top of the chart cupboard behind the planesmen, watching the depth gauges over their heads.

"Boat at periscope depth, sir."

Korth stands beside him, reading the instruments. "Thanks, so I see." Then he climbs the vertical ladder to where, above the control room, the attack periscope is housed.

"Up periscope." Korth takes a first, all-round look. "Higher." He searches again, more carefully. It is bright daylight now, horizon excellent. On all sides the sea stretches blank and bare to join the gleaming sky. Nothing stirring! And the propeller noises?

"Down periscope. Stand by to surface." The lookouts gather beneath the conning-tower hatch, ready to go aloft.

"Surface." The chief keeps his eye on the depth gauges: 30 feet—28—25—20— "Conning tower clear, sir."

"Blow out main ballast by Diesel."[1] The order is passed from man to man, down to the engine room. The starboard engine is started, and for a second of two it is allowed to suck in air from the hull, reducing the pressure to that of the atmosphere outside. Then the conning-tower hatch springs open,

[1] "Blow out main ballast by Diesel." When a submarine surfaces, high-pressure air is released into the main ballast tanks, forcing the water out of holes in the bottom of the tanks, thereby giving the boat "positive buoyancy." As this H.P. air is extremely valuable and only a small quantity can be stored, only approximately one-third

Korth scrambles out, alone at first, onto the bridge. He looks carefully all around—many a time, the boat has had to dive again immediately—all clear. "Come up, the bridge party."

The lookouts clamber up and strain through their binoculars for the ship that can now be heard on bearing 240 degrees.

"Engines, full ahead, together. Steer two-four-O."

Now the port engine coughs and stutters into life, joining the other in their familiar, powerful song, while the bow steadies off on the new course and the boat surges forward, thrusting strongly through the seas.

The boatswain's mate is the first to see them fine on the port bow, two thread-thin masts, just visible over the wandering peaks of the waves.

Korth lets the U-boat fall off her course a little so that he can observe the masthead height, inclination, bearing and other details of the enemy, passing down the figures to the quartermaster making a plot at the chart table below. Meanwhile the lookouts maintain a sharp watch over their respective sectors; from now on, that will be half the battle.

Slowly, hour by hour, the masts come up. The watch is changed; the men who have been relieved devour their dinner, then drop exhausted, to sleep.

Now, through the binoculars, the freighter's funnels can be seen emerging above the horizon. She must have passed close by the U-boat in the early hours of the morning, before it was light. She is zigzagging now with long, obtuse-angled alterations. And she's fast, a typical lone hand, by the looks of her, just the sort they risk sending without escort.

The Commander is in no hurry to close in, watches her sailing on at constant speed in her regular zigs and zags, so that he can get an accurate plot of her mean course.

Night has come again before the U-boat has overhauled the

---

of the water is blown out in this way, enough to bring the upper conning-tower hatch above the surface.

At this point British and German practices diverge. The British open the hatch and blow out the tanks by the "low-pressure blower," a rotary compressor discharging direct into the tanks. The German method was to start one of the Diesels, allow it for a moment to reduce the excess air pressure in the boat before opening the hatch, its exhaust, meanwhile, directed via a cross-connection into the ballast tanks until they were blown clear.—*Translator*.

enemy and taken up station on the estimated line of her course. Then she dives once more.

"Stand by, torpedo tubes."

The chief engineer keeps the boat trimmed at periscope depth—it is not easy. She is in continuous movement and to prevent the superstructure from breaking surface, the planesmen must constantly adjust the angle of the planes to counter the effect of the swell. At the same time, the forward and after auxiliary ballast tanks have to be flooded or blown, to assist in keeping the boat level in the water. Among the confusion of valve levers in the control room, the right ones have to be flicked over with lightning speed.

In the conning tower, Korth crouches at the lens of the attack periscope. Meanwhile, the torpedoes are in the tubes, the tubes have been flooded, the bow doors opened. It only remains to adjust the settings for speed, course and depth according to the figures given by the Commander.

The freighter is coming closer and closer, her outline growing steadily. Now Korth can see the whole ship. She is small indeed, smaller even than he had suspected. She seems to be in an extraordinary hurry and now and again as she churns on through the long swell, her stern is lifted clean out of the water and her screws revolve in mid-air. The bow dips, as if crouching for a stupendous leap, then rears up steeply, shredding the seas, then plunges again with massive deliberation, scattering showers of spray.

So that the torpedo will not pass under the target, Korth has the setting adjusted to an even shallower depth.

"Up periscope." He takes a quick look, orders a slight change of course. That ought to do it.

"Down periscope. Group down, slow together."

Two minutes before the sights come on! One torpedo only, the target isn't worth more. Suppose she zigs again, before—

"Up periscope." No, there she comes.

"Down periscope." Ninety seconds . . . eighty . . . seventy . . . one last look, to make sure.

"Up periscope." Fine! Only five degrees off the firing angle.

"Stand by, tube three. *Achtung*. Here she comes, her bow just visible.

"*Rohr drei*, LLOSSS!" The hand firing-lever in the conning tower is thrown over, a bell shrills out and with a soft hiss, the compressed air drives the torpedo from its tube.

"Torpedo running!" comes from the hydrophones, while in the control room the vents are opened to flood the trimming tank in the bow, compensating for the loss of the torpedo's weight.

Now all is silence. All those not immediately required at their action stations hover round the hydrophone operator waiting for the sound of the explosion. The P.O. telegraphist stands crouched over his stop-watch, following the thin needle as it jerks round the dial to time the torpedo's run, so that the actual range can be compared with the Commander's estimate.

"Up periscope." At any moment the fountain of water should spurt up against the steamer's side. From the conning tower, Korth hears: "Torpedo still running!" then the bearings of its propeller-sounds as it streaks up to the target. The two sounds—the ship's and the torpedo's—are rapidly converging now, and—(For a split second, the P.O.'s eyes leave the stop watch and glance at the Commander: "Well—?") and—they've crossed! They're separating—still separating, wider and wider. They're wandering away. . . .

"Down periscope."

And now what? Another go? The whole laborious process to be repeated? Wait till she's out of sight, surface, set after her again, working round until once more the U-boat lies in her path? Yes, but not for another torpedo attack.

"Isn't worth it, lad." Korth answers a sailor's unspoken question. "We'll try with the gun, tonight."

Korth waits till the freighter is well past, surfaces, and follows, keeping touch, just out of sight.

Meanwhile, after the days of storm, the silk-blue sea spreads undulating gently, to join an almost cloudless sky far off along the clear-cut seam of the horizon. Closer at hand the water glistens darkly, with here and there a flicker of green. As she cuts into the long Atlantic swell, the U-boat throws up a double furrow of curving white foam, then the bow heaves clear again in a shower of glittering prisms and sinks once more under the massive, slanting seas.

At regular intervals, as the freighter reaches the farthest point on one of her tacks, the lookouts see the faint wisp of her funnel smoke far ahead on the starboard horizon. Each time, they wait tensely, wondering whether it will appear again, knowing that if she keeps to her route in zigs and zags she cannot escape her doom.

In the late afternoon, far off on the bow, a plane is sighted. Dive? No. Korth decides to wait, certain that at that distance, the U-boat has not been observed. The little dot turns toward the freighter, seen at that moment as a faint smudge above the waves, comes lower, then starts to drop steeply down—a German plane on long-distance reconnaissance? Soon after, the hydrophones pick up three loud explosions. The dot climbs up again, then dwindles away into the sky— and there, still visible, is the freighter's funnel smoke, exactly as before, while the ship, implacable as a tank, continues undeterred on her methodical zigzag course.

But soon Korth notices a change. The enemy has decided to increase speed a little. In answer, the U-boat drives harder through the seas, torrents of water swamping and sousing the lookouts on the bridge. But now all thought of abandoning the quarry is dismissed. It has become a point of honor to send the ship to the bottom.

Night falls, with bright moonlight. She is visible as a vague shadow now, gliding between the sea and the stars, still on the same bearing and following a straight course at a slightly reduced speed—strangely sure of herself!

Korth evolves his plan of attack. With a bright moon and the U-boat in continual motion, a gun battle is going to be a risky undertaking. He tries out the boat in different positions in relation to the seas and the moon, selecting the most favorable. To make detection more difficult, the boat must lie against the darkest segment of the horizon, yet the moon must not be shining on the side of the hull which is nearest to the enemy. At the same time, the boat must lie as quietly as possible in the swell, otherwise, with the seas breaking continually over them, the crew may not be able to serve the gun, let alone to achieve any hits.

Having made his decision, the Commander orders: "Gun action!" The men drop down onto the casing, choose a moment when the hull is clear of a trough and the bow is rising again to dart forward and strap themselves swiftly to the gun, throw open the breech, train the barrel—a sea sweeps surging over them and they are left struggling, waist-high in water— then steady themselves for the "open fire."

Closing in, Korth keeps the freighter fine on his bow, so as to remain for as long as possible unseen. Standing beside him on the bridge, the gunnery officer waits tensely for the order to fire.

Range 1,875 yards—in the bright moonlight, the shadow of the enemy ship grows steadily larger, the dark shaft of the gun-barrel following silently, pointing at her heart.

Twelve hundred and fifty yards. "Open fire!" Immediately, the gunnery officer repeats the order to the crew and on the deck below the boatswain rips at the firing lanyard.

Nothing happens. . . .

A dud! Swearing, the men eject and load in another shell. Another sea comes gurgling up and again the crew are left hanging in their straps. They wait their moment, then, silence—

"What the hell's going on down there?" roars the gunnery officer from the bridge.

"Another dud!"

Suddenly, from the freighter comes a double flash and two 40-millimeter guns bark out. They've spotted the U-boat.

"Hard-a-port. Engines, half-speed ahead, together. Now the 20-millimeter," yells Korth. The Oerlikon sputters from its platform behind the bridge, chasing its flaming mice across to the enemy, to the point where the flashes were seen. The freighter sheers off, but can still be seen in the binoculars and followed. She is alert now and ready for the attack to be resumed.

"What's wrong with that cannon?" The gunnery officer has jumped down beside the crew. It appears that the fat smeared thickly over the gun to protect it from the salt water has partly solidified, jamming the firing pin. The trouble is easy to cure.

Meanwhile, the wireless operator has picked up an SOS from the steamer in which she gives her name. The Register lists her as one of the fast meat freighters, built just before the war for the North Sea run, maximum speed 14 knots.

But her real maximum is more like 17, and she's doing it now—and reeling off, as well, all the tricks and dodges that a really fast lady can play. She needs watching every second. Suddenly, she puts the helm hard over, turns through 180 degrees and goes off again in the opposite direction. But Korth spots her in time and the U-boat clings desperately to her heels.

At last the moon, waxed almost to full, goes down and soon it will be day. Now the gun has been regreased and is ready for action again. The boat can close in to attack, once more bow-on so that the enemy cannot bring his guns to bear.

The range is still over 3,000 yards when the U-boat is spotted. Immediately, the freighter turns sharply away. The fight is on; this time, it must be to a finish!

With a roar, the U-boat's 88-mm. opens fire, fotoflashing the conning tower and the faces on the bridge—and again, "Fire!"

A hit—*Donnerwetter! Gut!*

A moment's pause, till the boat is on an even keel again, then the third shot goes sailing over.

A fantastic business, this, trying to fire a gun from the deck of a small submarine, cavorting in a heavy Atlantic swell, while the seas fling and knock you about, till only your safety belt saves you from going overboard! Yet, only five shots with incendiary at the enemy's bridge, at over 2,500 yards, at night, and four of them are hits—some shooting! Three times the U-boat crosses the freighter's bows and the gun is kept on the target. The men had really got down to it, they are doing some lovely shooting now. Already the bridge over there is a mass of flames.

At last, as she turns away, the freighter's two guns can be brought to bear. Then the German Oerlikon goes after them again. In quick succession, the shells of the 88-millimeter crash into the hull.

Soon the freighter is out of control and her guns are silent. The crew take to the boats and row away from the ship. Korth brings the U-boat into the most favorable position and the 88-mm. shoots on, unchallenged now, into the abandoned wreck, putting a couple of high explosives into her at the water-line. Flames burst up from her hull, casting a red glare over the steam that is pouring from her engines. She slumps by the stern and starts to settle down.

The gunnery officer orders "cease fire."

Then a last shot goes rumbling over.

"You! Jackass, down there. Can't you hear me? I said cease fire."

Now the retching crack of the Oerlikon and the roar of the heavier gun have ceased and silence sings in the ears. Then, gradually, from across the water, the men hear another sound:

the crackling of the flames as they curl up over the dying ship.

The gun is made fast, the shells are manhandled back down the hatch and then, soaked to the skin, exhausted, but grinning all over their faces, the men go below to strip off their sea-togs and answer their messmates' questions.

"Coxswain, a bottle of schnaps for the gun's crew!" As they pass him, swinging themselves down the hatch, the sailors grin back at their Commander. A-h! a bright idea of the Old Man's, that was! "And he said, let the rest of the lads come up one by one," they tell them below, "that's what he said!"

The Old Man is like a father, thinking of everybody. How seldom the crew get a chance to see the result of their efforts, an enemy ship stricken and sinking! So now, up they go to the bridge, the chief engineer, then the P.O. telegraphist, then, after a while, the E.R.A.s, the wireless operators, the stokers, the torpedomen (the "Mixers" as they are called) and all whose duties keep them normally at their stations below. One by one, they stand, watching the fearful sight. . . .

The flames are still licking up out of the wreck, her sides glowing red with the heat. The bridge and superstructure have long since collapsed, a billowing sea of sparks shooting high up into the dawn-streaked sky. Now the bow rears steeply up, and then, slowly but gathering speed, the doomed ship slips, hissing and groaning, stern first, to her grave.

Korth watches silently, numbed. Three times that bold little ship escaped him. Now she has met her fate, here in the cold gray wastes of the Atlantic beneath the icy, pitiless stars. The seas closed over her as if she had never been. How long will they continue to bear me up, he wonders, how long before it is our turn?

6 IN ENEMY HANDS

In March 1941 Germany lost three outstanding U-Boat Commanders: Prien (U.47), Kretschmer, (U.99) and Schepke (U.100). The U.99 and the U.100 were sunk while attacking the same convoy on March 17. Schepke was killed, Kretschmer taken prisoner. "Few U-Boat commanders were their equals in ruthless ability and daring."[1] This is the story of Otto Kretschmer, *Translator.*

At about 3:30 a.m. on March 17, 1941, the wireless operator of a U-boat in mid-Atlantic picked up faint signals on the

[1] Sir Winston Churchill, *The Second World War.*

inter-service wave-length. It was a message from the U.99:
"Destroyer depth-charged; 50,000 GRT; prisoner of war. U-
Kretschmer."

Kretschmer announcing his own captivity! How did it come
about?

Earlier that night he had been in the middle of a British
convoy off the Faroes, two hundred miles northwest of the
Shetland Islands. He had fired all his torpedoes, claiming victims with some—hence the "50,000 gross register tons" in his
signal—and was disengaging now to return to base at St.
Nazaire.

The moon was in the south and Kretschmer headed northward where the horizon was darkest. Off Lousy Bank he was
expecting minefields—some drifting mines had already been
sighted—and he intended to keep it well on the starboard
beam.

The bridge watch consisted of four men, each with a lookout sector of ninety degrees: one officer, one P.O. and two
seamen. The officer had the additional duty of making a
periodic check on all sectors.

During one of these, when standing beside the P.O. he
caught sight of a gun turret shimmering in the moonlight,
a British destroyer at point-blank range not more than a hundred yards away. Perhaps the P.O. should have spotted her
earlier; perhaps out of the darkness she was suddenly there
without warning, like a chessman placed on a board. At any
rate, with the surprise and shock of seeing that apparition so
close at hand, the officer of the watch made a terrible mistake. Instead of following his own experience and his Commander's standing instruction—"When reacting to objects
sighted at night, stay surfaced"—he lost his head and gave the
order to dive. A moment later, he realized he had made a fatal
error. By then it was too late; the moment the flooding levers
had been pulled down in the control room, the fate of the
U-boat was sealed.

In fact, though she had been on the surface the U-boat had
not been sighted and her presence was only discovered later,
after she had dived and been located in the destroyer's hydrophones. But Kretschmer was hopeful of avoiding destruction.
Since the previous year, the exact depths at which depth
charges could be set to explode had been known to the German High Command; the greatest, for example, was at that

time 152 meters, or 498 feet. By submerging to some inter-
mediate depth, Kretschmer had hitherto escaped serious
damage.

This time he was unlucky. Almost immediately, the main
motors were put out of action. Water broke in through the
pressure hull. The U-boat started to slump down. He ordered
all tanks to be blown. She stopped sinking, then started to rise,
slowly, at first, then with increasing speed. At 260 feet, to
prevent her breaking surface, Kretschmer ordered the tanks to
be vented, but the upward impetus could not be checked;
having no steerage way, the boat would not react to the hydroplanes. So she came to the surface and, determined this time
to keep her there, Kretschmer once again ordered: "Blow
main ballast."

From the bridge he could see one destroyer stopped within
hailing distance on the beam and a second destroyer slowly
approaching the U-boat from the opposite quarter, apparently
on an H.E. bearing. If he had had torpedoes, he could have
sunk them both.

The first destroyer was the *Vanoc*. Since the previous fore-
noon, she had been trailing the U.100. Schepke's boat, and
had just that moment destroyed it. She was picking up survivors. The other destroyer, closing on the H.E. bearing, believed at first it was the U.100 she had located. Then when
they realized they had a second victim within their grasp, both
enemy ships started to deluge the U.99 with a hail of fire from
their 4.7-inch guns and 2-pounder multiple pom-poms.

Immediately, the U-boat heeled over and in case she should
take a sudden plunge, Kretschmer ordered all hands to the
upper deck, where they took cover under the lee of the conning-tower superstructure. Soon after, the engineer officer reported that the U-boat could no longer submerge. There was
now only one thing to do: abandon ship. All meanwhile having remained unwounded, Kretschmer ordered the men below
again so that they could collect the necessary personal gear.
Then Kretschmer made his signal and all secret documents
were destroyed.

The destroyers were firing with unabated fury and high-
pressure air was escaping from the ballast tanks through leaks
or started rivets in the hull. Suddenly the U-boat settled
deeper by the stern and, before it could be closed, the conning-tower hatch was underwater and seas were pouring down

into the boat. The boatswain standing by the galley hatch had the presence of mind to shut it before that, too, became submerged. He just managed to save himself from being swept overboard by clinging to the after jumping-wire.

The only men inside the boat were the first lieutenant and the engineer officer. The latter immediately opened all the blowing valves to lighten the boat with what remained of the high-pressure air. It sufficed to lift the stern, but not the conning-tower hatch, which remained below the surface. The two officers then fought their way upward against the inrushing seas until, their arms emerging above water, they were hauled through the hatch by the men on the upper deck.

By now, realizing that the U-boat was crippled, the destroyers had slackened fire. Those of the crew who had been on the after casing when the stern submerged had been washed overboard, but they clung together—as instructed for such emergencies—and were picked up by *Vanoc* over her scrambling nets.

Soon after, *Walker* came closer to starboard and lowered a boat. Watching closely the activities on the enemy ship, Kretschmer realized they were about to send a boarding party. If something was not done to hasten her end, they might capture the U-boat before she went down. The engineer officer suggested venting aft so that she could go stern-first. Kretschmer agreed, telling him to loosen the valves only a fraction on their seatings. The engineer went below and soon the air started to roar out of the tanks.

The next second the bows reared up, the periscope struck backward onto the water and the U-boat had gone, taking the engineer with her; only a great patch of oil and survivors struggling in the water showed the place where she had been a moment before.

Kretschmer had been standing by the conning-tower hatch, waiting to give his officer a hand-up. Suddenly a great surge of water had swept him clean off his feet and the next moment he found himself swimming among the rest of his crew.

Walker headed toward them and the crew were helped up over the side; they no longer had the strength to climb the scrambling nets alone. Two men were missing. Perhaps they had succumbed to exhaustion, perhaps to the cold: at that time of year, between the Faroes and Iceland, the sea was icy.

Kretschmer waited till last before allowing himself to be helped on board.

He was then taken to the captain's cabin, given a change of clothes, a handkerchief, blankets and told to help himself to cigarettes and a drink. As soon as he had changed he fell into a deep sleep. The last thing he remembered was seeing a sailor posted at the doorway, a pistol at his side.

He woke up to find the destroyer captain facing him, sitting on the edge of the desk. Kretschmer congratulated the captain: the captain expressed tactful condolence. The atmosphere was markedly courteous. The senior engineer came to see him. "How do you manage to pass the time?" "I am trying to read, but not succeeding very well. I find it difficult to concentrate. . . ." Later the officer returned bringing a jigsaw puzzle.

The destroyer had some merchant skippers on board, earlier victims of Kretschmer's. They, too, came to see him and related without rancor how almost the entire convoy had been destroyed. They had all had to swim for it. They said they always carried their emergency kit with them when at sea.

The next evening Kretschmer played his first rubber of bridge.

When they reached Liverpool the prisoners were fetched by an army escort. After some hours in a military detention barracks they were taken to the station. Wherever they stopped on the way, the mob tried to get at them. Some picked up heavy lumps of rock, others, when they recognized the U-boat commander by his cap, gestured, drawing their fingers across their throats.

In due course the survivors of the U.99 found themselves in an interrogation center at Cockfosters, in Hertfordshire. The house lay in a large park, where the prisoners were allowed to take walks. A number of rooms were allotted to them, but the occupants of a room were never allowed to stay together for long. By moving them about it was hoped to keep the prisoners talking: no one seemed to mind the noise, on the contrary, special plywood ceilings seemed to have been installed to amplify the sounds.

With the men, the treatment varied in order to unsettle

them and make them more communicative. Intimidation was tried and some even were threatened with shooting.

Kretschmer himself was treated with every consideration. One day he was invited to tea and told during the course of the meal that he had been promoted to Korvettenkapitän. Apparently the news had been given out by the Deutscher Rundfunk.

A few days later he was issued civilian clothes and taken to London, to the Admiralty. There he was taken before Captain Creasy, the Director of Anti-Submarine Warfare.[1]

The Captain, it seemed, wanted to have a chat and a drink with him so that he could have a look at one of these U-boat officers for himself. He was very genial and well informed; he appeared to know most details of the U-99's Atlantic patrols. He was also skillful at slipping in questions on Service matters during the course of conversation. Kretschmer had to be continually on his guard in case he should say too much.

The interview left Kretschmer with an impression confirmed by later experience. The British were extremely well informed about the personal records of their opponents, knowing a surprisingly large number of them by name. To them, the U-boat Service was more than a label; it was a living entity. To us, on the other hand, the enemy was no more than an anonymous mass. Very few in Germany could have named the Director of Anti-submarine Warfare.

In the following year, Kretschmer was sent to Canada, to a P.O.W. camp at Bowmanville, on the shores of Lake Ontario. It included in its amenities a swimming pool and a gymnasium. The prisoners constructed a sports ground for themselves.

While at Bowmanville, the Germans established secret communication with the outside world by means of a simple code which they used in the letters home, and later one of the prisoners, a Luftwaffe physics instructor, succeeded in building a wireless transmitting and receiving set. The receiver was in constant use, on one occasion even picking up an SOS from a German blockade-runner off Tristian da Cunha in the South Atlantic.

The transmitter came into use when the ambitious idea was conceived of asking Admiral Dönitz whether a rescue by

[1] Later Admiral Sir George Creasy, K.C.B., C.B.E., D.S.O., M.V.O., Commander-in-Chief, Home Fleet.—*Translator.*

U-boat would be possible from the east coast of Canada. Dönitz answered yes.

The next difficulty was to find a suitable spot to suggest for the rendezvous. The atlas finally revealed one that could be reached both by the U-boat from the east and the escapees from the west: Maisonette Point, in Chaleur Bay, in the estuary of the St. Lawrence.

Dönitz accepted this point as the rendezvous and signaled that each night for a week at the new moon a U-boat would appear off Maisonette Point.

Meanwhile foreign currency arrived from Germany in double-bottom tins, with cypher-keys, maps and other escape material. It was planned to make a mass escape by tunnel. The first tunnel collapsed when only half finished. A second was started. It had to cover a distance of 230 feet, and for almost a year the work went on under the noses of the guards and despite repeated security checks by the camp staff.

Every grain of earth had to be disposed of in order not to betray the scheme. It was stowed away between the double ceilings in the living quarters. Sometimes they would collapse under the weight—they were only made of cork—and then the whole would have to be repaired, the ceiling repainted and all suspicious traces removed in the course of a single night. Air circulators were constructed for the men working at the tunnel face, wooden trucks for carrying away the spoil and water pumps in case of flooding.

Throughout this period, the prisoners' life started after dark, when the whole camp would begin to seethe with subterranean activity. One night repairs were being made to a damaged ceiling. To reach it a pyramid of furniture had been built up on the floor. It collapsed with a fearful crash, bringing the guards into the camp, and with that the whole scheme was discovered.

Though the mass escape was now impossible, one officer, Kapitänleutnant Heida, succeeded in escaping from the camp during the week when the U-boat was to be at the rendezvous. He scaled an electricity pylon inside the perimeter with climbing irons and then hauled himself hand-over-hand in a home-made boatswain's chair over the cables leading to another pylon on the far side. Dressed in Canadian uniform and equipped with forged identity papers and the necessary currency, he first went to Montreal to buy himself a pocket flashlight and then proceeded to Maisonette Point. He found it covered with Canadian troops under canvas. He was stopped, but after checking his papers they let him go. He was stopped again as he was trying to work his way round the tents, and this time he was arrested.

Meanwhile, the U-boat had entered Chaleur Bay. She was heading toward Maisonette Point when four corvettes suddenly appeared and gave chase. Though the commander succeeded in bringing her out, it was clear that the Canadians had discovered the plan.

Thereafter, there were few successful escapes from Camp Bowmanville, and it was not until 1948 that Kretschmer himself reached home, after being a prisoner for seven years.

7 POPPA SMELLS A RAT

ON HIS second patrol as commander of the 740-ton U.106, Kapitänleutnant Hessler took a trip to the South Atlantic, as the U-boat man would say, lying in wait for British shipping off Freetown.

At that time, Freetown was one of the most frequented harbors on the West African coast, the fast ships sailing singly round the Cape to Britain and the big convoys usually stopping there to refuel. Though German U-boats had only recently been operating in the area, which was so far removed from their bases, it was one that offered plenty of opportunities.

On Sunday, June 1, 1941, the log of the U.106 recorded: "Wind west, Force 2. Sea calm with slight swell. To the east, in the direction of Africa, a haze like thick soup. . . ."

Inside the U-boat the heat was colossal, and though on the bridge there was a light breeze, the sun's rays scorched the skin.

Suddenly out of the red-brown haze the masts of a steamer appeared. The U-boat had the sun behind her, and as he closed with the enemy Hessler was able to remain unobserved. But it was no easy task. No sooner had they been sighted than the masts disappeared, then came once more into view as the U-boat altered course. Hessler managed to close a little before the enemy turned and made off; then back he came again. Was the skipper over there mad, wondered the U-boat commander, or more cunning than the Old Gooseberry himself?

For over an hour Hessler and his coxswain watched this strange performance, trying to discover the enemy's intention and plot his mean course so that they could set their own course to intercept him. But try as they might, they could find no system in his zig zags; both in timing and direction, they seemed completely haphazard. He was apparently in no hurry to get anywhere.

At the chart table in the control room, the coxswain was tearing his hair out at the crisscross of lines and angles which represented the enemy's antics. It was a mystery to him how the fellow himself could make sense of them. One thing was certain: no Neutral would behave like that. A Neutral would sail on a straight course with a clear conscience and get his voyage as quickly as possible behind him.

This must be a Britisher. But even so, to think the time well spent waltzing about the ocean for the sake of added security against torpedo attack, here, at this distance from the U-boats' normal hunting-grounds! Odd, indeed. . . .

After an hour of this wild goose chase, Hessler could go to periscope depth and hope to get a closer look at the enemy. By that time the crew were tense with excitement. All but the new hands could tell from the rapid succession of orders to helm and engine room that it had not been easy to reach an attack position, that it was an old campaigner they had got in their sights this time.

The U.106 had three torpedoes left. As her commander on two patrols, Hessler had so far put 96,000 tons in the locker. Another 4,000 with the three remaining fish and he could go home. But was she 4,000 tons, this strange ship?

Hessler was just about to submerge when the steamer performed another of her sharp, unpremeditated turns. Swearing, he ordered the motors to full speed and tried to close in again. (The night before, he had lost at Skat; that had usually been a good sign!) At last he had the enemy beam-on in the periscope.

Whenever conditions allowed he would give the crew a running commentary over the broadcasting system and now they heard: "Poppa can see something!" The high speed had been no joke for the crew. With the heat from the motor room, the temperature in the boat had risen to 122° F., and that in tropical humidity. But now they began to revive. What could he see, the Old Man? The steamer?

"Poppa can see a gun!"

A great groan of relief went up. The ship was armed, so they could attack her without more ado. No boarding party needed, no examination of ship's papers. No "harmless" American to be left, perforce, untouched while her wireless reported the U-boat's position.

"A motor-ship," the Commander continued, "a good three thousand tons!"

Only three thousand? That wouldn't make up their hundred-thousand. And if it took all three torpedoes to sink her, what then?

"Poppa says two torpedoes; that's all she'll get. We must keep one in reserve."

Hessler ordered the high-power periscope to be raised so that he could examine the enemy in more detail, then he put his eyes to the lens, pressing his forehead against the shell-shaped rubber buffer, jagged-edged, now, from the nervous plucking of his fingers during the tension of previous attacks.

After a moment: "Poppa sees nothing but harmless *matelots* . . ." came Hessler's voice again, "matelots in bedroom slippers." There was a roar of laughter from the crew at this impression of the seamen, lounging on the steamer's deck.

"Down periscope." Hessler ordered another slight change of course. In spite of her strange behavior, he had seen nothing unusual about the motor ship. A solitary gun in the poop, but all British ships had that now; a few colored seamen—Indians, possibly, drifting about, off duty, or leaning in bored attitudes over the rail; the skipper, pipe wedged in his mouth, sitting in a wing of the bridge, the picture of peace. And yet, those nervous, complicated evolutions . . .?

"Stand by, Three and Four Torpedo-tubes!" Then the figures for the torpedo settings, then a crackle through the voice pipe from the bow compartment, confirming that the order had been carried out: "All clear for submerged attack!"

"Up periscope." Enlarged in the powerful lens, the steamer's every detail could be clearly seen. Hessler had outmaneuvered her, was now in an ideal position for attack. The bridge was coming into the crosswires:

"Stand by." (Still, over there, the skipper sat on, drowsing over his pipe.)

"Fire Three! Fire Four!"

Almost together, the torpedoes went surging from their

tubes. Immediately, in the control room the torpedo-gunner's mate opened the flooding-valves to restore the trim and the water went booming into the tanks. At the periscope, Hessler watched, fingers plucking at the rubber eye shield. . . .

One of the torpedoes was a surface-breaker, would inevitably be spotted as it went spluttering and hissing toward its prey. Sure enough, in a moment the somnolent company leaped suddenly into life, somebody began frenziedly waving his arms, the skipper shot up from his chair—all too late.

The range was short and as the ship began to turn the first waterspout reared, glittering against her side, and almost at the same spot, the second, before the first had time to descend. Then two massive explosions came rumbling over the water and as the vast mushroom of spray dropped back into the sea, a dense explosion cloud swept billowing up into the air, carrying with it the shattered fragments of lifeboats and other wreckage. A moment later the stern was enveloped in fire, steam and smoke, and all that remained in view was a cavernous hole in the steamer's side, at least thirty feet high by thirty feet broad.

As the water poured in, the steamer heeled over, losing way, and finally came to a stop with a heavy list to starboard. And then, surprisingly, she sank no farther.

Coming up to within seventy feet of her stern, Hessler read the name and found her tonnage was given in Lloyd's Register as 4,020—just enough, after all, to complete his hundred-thousand! On the deck he could distinguish clearly her 105 mm. and 76 mm. A.A. guns, rendered useless now by the heavy list. All the same, he stayed at periscope-depth.

Out of his sight, on the higher port side, an abandon ship seemed to be in progress. He rounded the stern and found three lifeboats were being lowered, grinding, as they hung from their falls, along the listed side of the ship into the water. Then the crew followed, slithering down the plates on the seats of their trousers. Once in the water they began to swim for the boats, all of which had suffered considerable damage during their descent.

An astonishingly large crew the ship seemed to possess! More and more of them kept scrambling up over the rail and going down the side. Hessler started to count; there were eighty of them in the water alone, swimming after the lifeboats, apart from the ones going over the—

Now, what on earth—?

Hessler looked again, more closely, to make sure—yes, they were! In complete contrast with the scruffy, lounging figures seen earlier at the ship's rail, every man-Jack now appearing was dressed in spotless white uniform!

Now more cautious than ever, Hessler continued to circle the wreck of the enemy ship, trying to find a clue to this further mystery. Like every commander, he had heard plenty of tales of the British U-boat traps in the first world war, Q-ships, they had called them. . . .

Meanwhile, the water that had broken into the ship must have dispersed evenly through the hull, for settling slightly deeper in the water she had righted herself again and now lay on an even keel—with a hole like a barn-door in her side! She must be carrying a cargo of cork, or empty barrels, perhaps.

Still searching through the periscope, Hessler then noticed that in the superstructure of the flag deck there were a series of slits. As he watched, he could have sworn that one of them opened a little, then closed again, like a venetian blind. A moment later, on the bridge, he caught sight of a curious-looking pole, short and stubby, like a—it was, it was turning —a periscope!

In the U.106, Hessler continued his commentary to the crew: "There's a *matelot* hidden on the bridge over there, watching us. Poppa doesn't like this kettle of fish, it stinks!"

Those guns abandoned on deck—were they all? Or were other much more dangerous guns yet to be revealed, their crews closed up and waiting?

Hessler was now less than ever inclined to surface and put it to the test. That would be to play into the enemy's hands. Many a U-boat, he knew, had been caught that way in the first world war, had surfaced to finish off the enemy with gunfire (cheaper than torpedoes) and then suddenly flaps had dropped from the side of the "abandoned" ship, a row of gleaming barrels had appeared, then a withering broadside. . . .

And what were those strange-looking crates on the upper deck, wondered Hessler, like square wooden huts, battened down with tarpaulins? What did they conceal? Hessler had already been waiting half an hour, and meanwhile the ship would certainly have reported his position by radio. Aircraft from Freetown might turn up at any moment.

So he fired his last torpedo, from the starboard side, aiming at the forecastle, directly below one of the wooden crates. The explosion blew it 150 feet straight up into the air, then it came crashing down again, almost on top of the 6-inch gun it had been concealing. There had been six of those crates in addition to a dozen quick-firing 40-millimeters and row upon row of depth charges. The Q-ship laid bare her mysteries, as heeling to starboard ever more rapidly, she finally plunged stem first beneath the sea.

But first, as Hessler expected, yet more figures had appeared from nowhere and jumped overboard, swimming toward the three remaining boats; they, too, dressed from head to foot in impeccable white uniforms.

The explanation? It was a Sunday and, as in all British warships, in conjunction with Divine Service, the weekly Divisions, or mustering of the whole ship's company, had been held. With the sudden heeling of the ship under the impact of two torpedoes, the carefully prepared plans had been thrown into confusion. Instead of a dozen or so scruffy-looking lascars abandoning ship as the "panic party," while the real crew remained behind in concealment, a portion of the latter had been ordered to abandon ship as well.

The remainder then waited, in the hope that the U-boat would surface, so that they could bring their 6-inch guns to bear. But they waited in vain, for as Hessler's running commentary to his crew concluded:

"They were smart, but Poppa, this time, was smarter!"

8 YOUTH AT THE HELM

JOHANNES MOHR—or "Jochen," as he was called, to distinguish him from others of the same name—was the youngest commander in the Service. In his boat, the U.124, he sailed for eighteen months until on his sixth patrol in April, 1943, he was killed.

In that time, he achieved great success, 44,000 tons on his first patrol, the cruiser *Dunedin* on his second, a whole fleet of tankers on his third, for he was a deadly shot with a torpedo and possessed, as a U-boat commander, the ideal qualities of daring, good judgment and intelligence, while, as a man, he had all the irresistible charm and vitality of youth.

This was his first patrol. . . .

As the last glimmer of daylight is fading from the October sky, the dark shape of the U.124 starts to thrust more strongly through the swell. With ponderous shocks, the massing seas strike up against the conning tower, shattering in an ice-sharp, hissing deluge over the shrouded figures of the lookouts, crouched like horsemen upon their rearing steeds.

Below them and from either side, comes the hollow snuffle of the induction valves sucking in air to the Diesels, while the whole boat vibrates with the savage roar of the engines, running at maximum speed. A strange tension grips the men, for somewhere in the darkness ahead, sailing toward St. George's Channel and the comparative safety of the Irish Sea, lies the huge convoy first spotted from the air four days ago, 600 miles due west of Cape Finisterre. Then there had been twenty-seven ships, escorted by a cruiser, two destroyers and four smaller vessels.

Last night, far out in the Bay of Biscay, the U.124 descended, a lone wolf, on the fold and sank a great 12,000-ton tanker with two torpedoes, then made good her escape beneath the very nose of a destroyer toward the open seas. Since dawn, her commander has been trying to make contact again and at last the hydrophones have picked up the confused and distant sounds of the enemy propellers.

On the bridge the young Commander wedges himself, back to the weather, against the casing. Recently promoted and now above the tedium of watchkeeping, he grins maliciously at his less fortunate first lieutenant, then buries his mufflered chin deeper in the upturned collar of his oilskins.

A sudden gust of rain sweeps down from the night, dropping a curtain before the eyes of the lookouts. Mohr, his voice spluttering in the squall, begins to declaim the lines that he has ordained shall be recited from the bridge of the U.124 when storm is encountered:

> O woe is us, a storm is nigh!
> The clouds are bunching in the sky.
> Ceaselessly the rain doth fall,
> Wetting sheep and shepherd all!

The boat plows on into the seas and as the squall passes the lookouts crouch once more over their binoculars. Then comes a voice:

"Sir! Object, sir, approaching on the starboard bow!"

Mohr whips around, in time only to see a lean shape glide swiftly past and vanish astern—an enemy destroyer! This calls for caution or there may be some unpleasant surprises; one of those parachute flares, for instance, that the enemy looses off when he sniffs something suspicious on the wind.

Mohr alters course and speed a little. Hardly has he given the order than another shadow is sighted astern, this time a cruiser coming up, apparently, to change stations with the destroyer. (That's the way with these escorts; they dart off suddenly at a tangent from the convoy, exploring as the fancy takes them.) Of the other ships, there is still not a sign.

Mohr turns, deciding to follow the destroyer on the chance that it is now stationed astern of the convoy. And he's right; over there, dimly discernible against a lighter patch of sky, Mohr can just make out the shadows of three freighters.

The time is almost midnight.

One of the lookouts catches his eye. "Patience. When the destroyer allows the gap to widen for a moment, we can slip through."

Suddenly, the unmistakable sound of a torpedo exploding. That must be Mützelburg! Since nightfall, he, too, has been closing in; that much has been clear from the flow of signals coming up to the bridge from the wireless room.

At once the sky is festooned with flares and star-shells, most of them some distance from the U.124.

"Control room, slow ahead together. Port 15."

He lets the boat drop away to the west till the excitement is over. Hardly has darkness returned when Mohr closes in toward the destroyer stationed now on the starboard quarter of the convoy. The moment the enemy sheers to one side, the U-boat slips through the gap toward the merchantmen.

The long, long shadow of a huge tanker looms through the night. There's something really worth while! "Start the attack!" The shrill ring of the telegraphs becomes almost continuous while a stream of orders are passed to the helmsman and the engine room.

Bearings and range-angles are read off, transformed into details of the enemy's range, course and speed. A thrill of excitement runs through the crew, even the men in the motor room aft following feverishly, stage by stage, as the voices of the torpedo officer and the "mixers" in the bow torpedo compartment come past them in a series of tinny quacks through the voice pipe.

From the bridge the torpedo officer is just passing down the figures for the torpedo settings to be adjusted for running depth, course and speed. Then he bends over the night sight. The shadow of the tanker is coming into the crosswires.

Suddenly: "Hard-a-starboard!" The Commander's order to the helmsman roars out, breaking the spell, robbing the men of almost certain success, ruining everything. Why? Close, appallingly close, on the starboard beam, looms the shadow of a destroyer, bearing down on the U-boat for a certain collision. There's only one thing to do—give way at once, though another second and the torpedo would have left the tube.

The destroyer is on a reciprocal course to the convoy and instinctively the young Commander has chosen the more daring move, turning the bow to starboard, that is toward the destroyer, closing the angle at which the two ships are approaching. This will bring him nearer to the enemy than if he tried to escape by turning to port, but it also means that they will meet and pass in a very much shorter time. In those few moments there is a chance that the U-boat will remain unseen.

On the U-boat's bridge, the tension is almost unbearable. The destroyer comes up at breathtaking speed, her bow-waves like scimitars, poised above the knife-sharp prow.

"Clear the bridge!" The men obey immediately, plunging through the hatch, feet clear of the rungs and wait below. The U-boat is still within the enemy's circle of swing, where she can be rammed in the very act of diving. With hard, flickerless eyes, Mohr gauges the distance. It is a matter of seconds.

Seconds? More like minutes, it seems, since he gave the order and still the boat lies almost beam-on in the path of the advancing destroyer. Mohr grips the rim of the hatch cover, compelling himself to be calm.

With barely 350 yards between them, the U-boat begins to answer to the helm and now, as she swings, the distance is closing faster still. If the enemy turns to starboard by only a fraction, the U-boat will be rammed.

Alone, Mohr rides the plunging bridge, with senses strange-

ly clarified, aware of each smallest sight and sound. Three
hundred yards—a few moments only now. God, let him not
see; just this one second; and this one second more—

Mohr's thoughts flash to the forty-two men below, going
unconcerned and unsuspecting about their duties, to the three
lookouts from the bridge waiting at the bottom of the ladder,
not daring to breathe.

Back to the destroyer now, fine on the starboard bow, to
the U-boat, still turning toward her—the crew's, the boat's,
his own fate heaped in the scales.

Two hundred yards, and they're end-on, bow to bow.
The enemy continues, unswerving, on his course.

" 'Midships—steady!"

There! A sleek shadow gliding swiftly past, so close (130,
150 yards?), the Commander can see every detail of her
upperworks. . . .

But the U.124 remains unseen. They must be blind, all of
them, thinks Mohr. Can't they see the spray, bursting in a
fluff of white against the conning tower, the seas that foam
away from the casing as the bow plunges into the waves?
Can't they hear the odd, strange sound of the Diesels above
the rhythm of their own engines?

"Helm steady amidships, sir." Mohr bends over the hatch,
where he still stands, ready to jump down. "All clear!" he
roars, jovially, down the hatch. "Close up, the bridge party."

Immediately, the men start scrambling up the ladder, close
on each other's heels. Now the lookouts are once more closed
up, Mohr moves slowly away from the hatch, a curious dull-
ness suddenly pervading all his limbs. A few moments ago he
had felt a kind of rage that it should rest on him alone, the
responsibility for the fate of all. But it's a good thing, after
all, he thinks, that the men can remain in blissful ignorance
of what is really happening.

The roar of a depth charge sounds close by. The four men
on the bridge jump with the shock, the lookouts, only just
arrived, staring, amazement on their faces, at the Commander.
At last, the destroyer has spotted the wake of the U-boat and
is sowing it with depth charges.

Mohr takes up a course parallel to the convoy and moves
to the head in the hope of finding an opportunity there.

Now come the explosions of ten more depth charges,

farther away than the first. Are the Tommies getting nervous, trying to frighten off the U-boats that they cannot see? All around them, they sense well enough that there is danger waiting crouched and ready to spring, lurking everywhere in the dark recesses of the night.

Four more explosions, then there is silence, while the U.124 moves onward, thrusting through the seas. Where is that lovely tanker, Mohr wonders, that escaped him, and the other ships?

"Destroyer astern." At first, as the after lookout directs him, Mohr can see nothing. Yes, he can—there! Right astern, a suspicion of a shadow and now clearer, two shadows! Again Mohr clears the bridge, then hesitates, weighing up the chances. Stay on the surface? Or follow the others below, abandoning for the night all chance of further success?

"Full speed, plus ten." he calls after the cocooned figures of the lookouts, whose bulk still blocks the hatchway. "Ten more revolutions."

As he held the two shadows in the glasses, it looked as though they were not traveling so very much faster than the U-boat.

Bracing his legs Mohr steadies himself, and looks again. There they are, lying right astern. Have they seen us? He looks at them in turn, calmly, trying to judge: closer, definitely! Must he dive—more dangerous every second as the distance closes—and having dived, get a load of depth charges?

Let's try to get away as we are, showing him a slim silhouette! What's the distance now? Mohr takes a quick glance forward—all clear ahead.

To the helmsman: "Port five." No more; a sharp turn and the wash or some other change of aspect will be seen. But gently by degrees, the U-boat may be able to slip away.

Meanwhile, down below the bridge in the control room, the chief engineer, Oberleutnant (Ing.) Brinker, blows into the voice pipe to the engine room, then puts his ear to the mouthpiece. "Attention!" comes a voice. The chief talks to the engine-room E.R.A.—it must be like a turkish bath down there, with this continual running at full speed.

"Another ten revs?" roars the Obermachinist, making sure that his hearing is in order. "Right! Shall be done;—we'll do what we can. What's going on, then?" They'd like to be in the

picture down there, he and his men. Brinker bawls something
into the din—all that he himself knows, then steps back from
the pipe. All right, ten more revs, but that's the limit.

On the bridge Mohr watches the destroyers, first from one
side, then the other, gauging the distance. You've got to have
eyes like a lynx at this crazy speed, or you'll find yourself
running straight into the arms of some other warship. He can
see now the U-boat is falling a fraction off the line of the
destroyers' course. They have not spotted her yet, though the
distance is still slowly closing.

"Chief," he calls once again, down the hatch. "Ten more
revs. Maximum plus twenty."

In the opening of the lower hatch, two decks below, the
chief's upturned face appears, dimly visible in the reduced
light from the control room. "Can't be done. We're running
at maximum plus ten already."

Mohr bends down, fresh and unperturbed:

"Have a talk with those Diesels of yours, Brinker. Try a bit
of persuasion, because ten more revs I want and ten more
revs they must do."

The chief is about to answer, but already Mohr has vanished from the hatch and is standing aft again, straining
through his glasses. Brinker shrugs, then turns, grimacing, to
the voice pipe.

On the bridge Mohr stifles a sudden urge to laugh. What a
ludicrous situation this is—two destroyers on your heels and
no room to dive. The U-boat is moving, certainly, but they
can do twice her speed, any time they want; and they *will*
when they've spotted her. It's a very big risk for the sake of
staying surfaced and keeping in touch with the convoy.

Through the voice pipe, Chief talks to his E.R.A., telling
him by cunning adjustment to get the utmost ounce from his
engines.

"Here, Chief! Ten more revs! Maximum plus thirty; must
have them." Brinker hears the voice from the bridge before
the helmsman has time to repeat the order and springs to the
lower hatch: "To Commanding Officer!" he yells—Mohr's
face appears again at the opening above—"Man! At any moment the cylinder heads are going to blow clean out through
the pressure hull and onto the upper deck."

"Let them," Mohr laughs, completely unmoved at the

prospect. "Let your old donkeys run themselves solid." Mohr is now in the best of moods, for he can see that the U-boat is beginning to draw away from her pursuers and if all goes well should be able to escape unseen on the surface.

With the shuddering of the two donkeys, the bridge is already vibrating like an indiarubber drawn across glass. Faster? Brinker shakes his head. They won't stand it even at their present speed if it continues much longer.

Still Mohr stays alone on the bridge and still the lookouts wait in their gleaming oilskins below, ready at any moment to go aloft. From time to time a shower of spray, and occasionally a whole sea, rains down on them through the open hatches.

Now the U-boat is drawing farther and farther ahead, sheering off the course of the destroyers. Mohr raises the glasses, searching astern. Where are they now? For a moment he can see nothing, then taking in a wider arc spots them on a fresh course, two faint shadows falling away on the starboard quarter. Mohr watches the destroyers as they recede and fade into the night. He looks at his watch; it is just ten minutes since they first appeared.

Now for that tanker! But first, and before ordering up the lookouts, Mohr goes to the hatch: "Chief," he calls. "Chief. Congratulations! Just outsteamed two British destroyers."

Quickly the joke is passed around among the crew. Few of them can have known what was happening, or why they were running at such speed, though all could tell from the thunder of the Diesels that they were traveling as never before.

Now they look at each other, grinning and pursing their lips—proud of the Old Man, proud of the U.124, proud of their narrow escape; in other words, mighty pleased with themselves!

But that was not the end of the affair; it was only the beginning, though the worst of the danger was over.

Having risked his boat and the lives of all those in her to the point of disaster, Mohr was now able to reap his reward. The giant tanker that he had so nearly sunk escaped him, but three smaller tankers and three other ships met their doom that same night at this hands—44,000 tons, and another steamer damaged, of 5,000 tons! Well might Admiral Dönitz signal to his youngest commander as he returned, after all torpedoes had been fired, from his first patrol: "You can go home now; you deserve it."

9 RASMUS, SPIRIT OF THE DEEP

It was in October, 1941, in bright sunshine, as he was sailing out of the Bay of Biscay on the third day of his first patrol as commander of the U.106 that Kapitänleutnant Hermann Rasch discovered that his entire bridge watch of one officer and three men had been swept overboard and lost.

There was a following sea, a real fine-weather sea, and a bright blue sky with white, bosomy clouds—the sort of weather that called for a doubly sharp lookout against enemy aircraft and submarines, particularly in this area, on the very doorstep of the U-boat bases on the French Atlantic coast.

The men on the bridge, the officer of the watch and the lookouts (a midshipman and two signalmen), were all men of experience, excellent seaman and no newcomers to the U.106. They had not strapped themselves to the casing so that if they had to clear the bridge for an air alarm there would be no delay and the U-boat could more quickly submerge. In the space of a single watch the wind had increased from Force 4 to Force 8, from a moderate breeze to a forty-mile-an-hour gale, whipping the gentle, idling swell into great spindrifted storm waves.

And there was a following sea—dangerous, always, if you are on the bridge of a small submarine, lying deep in the water and traveling at only moderate speed. Just as the boat is rearing steeply, losing way as she climbs up the back of one sea, she can be overtaken by the next and sometimes she carries right under.

It was up to the men on the bridge, of course, to decide which was the greater danger, the menace from the air or the violence of the elements. Lulled, perhaps, by the lazy innocence of the sunshine, they decided they would wait for a while before strapping themselves to the casing.

It must have been the first great sea that took them, swelling up sudden and unexpected from astern, surging over bridge and conning tower, sweeping implacably on, wrenching their fists from the rails. . . .

In the conning tower, immediately below the bridge, the

helmsman had been finding it difficult in the steadily mounting seas to keep the U-boat to the course that had been called down to him from the bridge a short while before by the officer of the watch. Then, the upper conning-tower hatch had been shut (as always when too much water was being shipped) and the helmsman had been content to hear no more. He had been given his course and all else he wanted to know could be read from his instruments. Not until three-quarters of an hour later, when one of the wireless operators from the control room had reason to go up to the bridge, was it discovered that the U-boat had been sailing, blind and at the mercy of the enemy, on a set course alone through the raging seas.

For eight hours the Commander searched and scoured the area, knowing as he did so that it was pointless. In such seas and wearing seaboots and oilskins, the men wouldn't have stood a chance. Rasmus, the salt sea, had snatched them away in their unguarded moment and would not give them up.

After the search had been abandoned, Rasch called the ship's company one by one to the control room and told them what had happened. He pointed out the burden that the loss of the four men would place on the rest of the crew. Should he break off the patrol? From each man came the immediate and emphatic answer—carry on.

So the Commander, normally excluded from watchkeeping so as to be fresh for an emergency, took over the third watch, divided out the four men's duties among the crew, and detailed torpedomen, whose work did not involve long spells, to take the place of the vanished lookouts. They proved to be excellent.

Then the boat sailed on toward her billet, Rasch hoping for an early success to restore the morale of the crew. All seafaring men have their superstitions, and the tragedy—the only one of its kind on record—had been the greater shock for coming at the start of their commander's first patrol. But in war a U-boat can be successful only if her crew possess the spirit of attack and, no less important, the confidence which all submariners must have in themselves and their ability to overcome the hazards of their life.

Soon, as it happened, the U.106 came upon a lone ship and in such favorable circumstances that there was no difficulty in sinking her. A little while later a signal was received giving news of a fast and heavily escorted convoy on its way across the Atlantic probably heading for Newfoundland.

Though the convoy's position and course did not favor the attempt, Rasch immediately decided he would try to reach it. It would take at least two and a half, probably three, days of full speed and heavy fuel consumption and even then there would be only two nights in which to attack before the convoy reached the protection of the coast.

After he and the navigator had made the necessary calculations at the chart table, Rasch ordered full speed and brought the U-boat onto her new course.

Thanks to excellent contact reports supplied by other U-boats shadowing the convoy, Rasch was able to allow for every change in its mean course and though the convoy was making an average speed of 11 knots, on the evening of the third day a broad smoke streamer was sighted on the horizon. If he wanted to attack that night, there was no time for him to reach the head of the convoy. All he could hope to do— and that was hard enough with moonlight and the sea as placid as a pond—was to break in from the less favorable position astern.

He decided to wait till the moon went down before closing in. Meanwhile the ships, circled continually by a large number of escorts, were proceeding calmly on their way; it looked as though the other U-boats, whose reports had led him thus far, had not yet made an attack. But Rasch knew they were old hands at the game, wary, taking their time. Would he, the newcomer, be able to get in before them?

Hardly had darkness fallen when a wild crisscross of star-shells suddenly lit up the sky some distance away on the port quarter. Did that mean the convoy had altered course, away from him? Rasch hesitated, wondering whether he should turn southward toward them. Then, as no sound of explosions followed, he decided to continue to the northwest, on the chance that the firework display was a bluff. If his calculations were correct, that would bring him on to the mean course of the convoy.

Rasch ordered "Stand by, action stations," and calling again for full speed, set forward into the dark. He was approaching the Newfoundland Bank, notorious for its fogs. In the damp, heavy atmosphere, visibility was barely 300 yards. Beyond that all lay hidden in the sodden blanket of night.

For a good two hours, Rasch pressed on, almost blind, trusting to his nose. Then he went below to brood again over his charts. With the dividers he plotted the distances that the convoy could meanwhile have covered, so obtaining the area in which it should now be found and the courses on which to continue the search—then to the bridge once more to join the lookouts.

Still the boat thrust onward through the fog, the bow wave as steady in the dead-calm sea as the twin tufts of a beard. Was it, after all, a will-o'-the-wisp they were chasing?

"All the same—" Rasch turned to his torpedo officer who was peering into the eddying night—"I wouldn't mind betting they're here somewhere."

"Sir!" broke in one of the lookouts. "Must be smoke about sir. This fog smells like Leipzig Station."

The man was right. Twenty minutes later the fog suddenly lifted and with visibility now at 2,000 yards Rasch found himself in the middle of the convoy. Immediately ahead was a fat bunch of tankers, zigzagging irregularly. Rasch would have to mount a separate attack for each.

First he made for a 9,000-tonner, closing astern then turning sharply at 350 yards to fire two torpedoes. The ship blew up and disintegrated, falling literally about its attackers' ears.

Immediately he had fired, before even the ship was hit, Rasch had turned to search for the next one, knowing that at any moment the warships would be upon him. Another tanker loomed into view—another attack (A-torpedoes, this time, driven by compressed air, aimed off on the director angle to allow for the tanker's speed). Rasch could see them clearly as they went streaking toward the target and so could the tanker, for suddenly her propeller-wash foamed up as the engines were put to full speed astern.

The tanker began to lose way while the torpedoes were still running and Rasch watched them surge on and pass ahead of her, within a few feet of her bow. Meanwhile her guns were manned and she opened fire with tracer. Rasch started to turn the U-boat to bring the after torpedo tube to bear.

At that moment he sighted two slim shadows racing toward him, their bow waves like giant wings: destroyers!

"D-I-V-E." Heels upon heads, the lookouts jumped clean down the conning tower and the Commander hadn't even time to shut the hatch before the air was hissing raucously out of the tanks.

The chief engineer, a wily hand with fourteen patrols to his credit, had already sized up the situation from what he could see and hear in the control room and acted on his own initiative. Anticipating the order to dive (strictly against regulations!) he had already partially flooded all but the after ballast tank and now, without waiting for each compartment to report "cleared for diving," his men were wrenching over the flooding levers and spinning the wheel valves to open the main vents, determined to dive the boat in record time.

Eighteen seconds after the Commander's order, the U.106 had submerged. At 60 feet, the first depth charges began to explode, fortunately not close, or she would have been torn wide open. Rasch went deeper, the boat was brought level and trimmed, all machinery stopped.

For nine hours the destroyers searched for the German with Asdic and hydrophones; for nine hours plastered him with depth charges. First the main fuses went: the emergency lighting was switched on. Then the dial glasses of the depth gauges were shivered. Water began spurting in forward and into the control room, until the outboard valves were closed. Then the valves started to loosen in their seatings: she was taking water rapidly. Aft, it reached the level of the propeller shafts and the bilge pumps had to be used or the boat would have become unmanageable. The noise was picked up and the depth charges came closer—but the seams in the pressure hull held.

After nine hours Rasch was able to creep away a little. The destroyers loosened their hold on the prey and went off to rejoin the convoy. At 14.00 hours the U-boat was able to surface. She was the only one that had attacked the convoy. The new Commander had sunk 9,000 tons.

10 ONE CHANCE IN A THOUSAND

Mid Atlantic, November 24, 1941. Heading southward into the tropical sun, the U.124, under her young Commander, Johannes Mohr, was sailing at leisurely speed through seas that were like liquid gold.

Dinner was just over, there had been rice pudding again,

the Commander's favorite dish. Petty officer Henning, the quartermaster of the relieving watch, scrambled out onto the bridge to take over duty as the forward lookout on the port side.

He had hardly put the glasses to his eyes when just visible between the peaks of the long Atlantic swell the tip of a mast emerged above the horizon. "Mast in sight, Red, O-four-five."

In a moment Mohr was on the bridge, sun helmet pushed back and glasses to his eyes.

Sure enough, the faint thread of a mast. "Engines full ahead together. Port fifteen, steer one-seven-O." The voice of the helmsman acknowledging, then the shrill clang of the engine-room telegraphs and the song of the Diesels swept into the major key.

Soon the distant thread revealed itself as a topmast, then a smaller, mainmast appeared—a warship.

Two days before, they had sighted their first ship since leaving base, an American cruiser. Cursing, they had had to let her go, knowing full well that as soon as they were spotted their position would be reported to the British. Would this turn out to be another American? Probably not. She was making a good 18 knots and was zigzagging in short, even legs, mean course northwest. If this continued the operation would be simple: an accurate plot of her course, the choice of a suitable point to lie in wait, and then the U-boat would be able to intercept and torpedo her from periscope depth. But first, she must be identified.

Ordering a further increase of speed, Mohr waited till the tops of the funnels were in view and then sent the bridge watch below lest their heads silhouetted against the skyline give the U-boat away.

Meanwhile, in case the ship should turn out to be British, the outer torpedo doors had been opened, flooding the tubes in readiness, and the torpedo settings had been provisionally adjusted to the figures given by the first lieutenant.

Within forty minutes of first sighting the warship, the U-boat was ready to go to periscope depth. On the Commander's order, the chief engineer, Oberleutnant Brinker, gave the necessary instructions to the outside E.R.A. and then stood in the control room, watching the gauges over the heads of the planesmen. Suddenly there was a crash of shattering glass and the chief and all around him were choking under a gush of seawater. A depth gauge had burst.

Immediately two men had to crawl into the bilges to try to block the inrush. Time was short. With the fore hydroplanes out of action, the U-boat had nevertheless to be kept perfectly trimmed or all possibility of torpedo attack would be gone. But the greatest danger was that the long fore-casing would break the surface and be spotted. It seemed almost impossible to prevent but, using only the after hydroplanes and the trimming tanks, Brinker succeeded in keeping the trim, and the boat remained ready for action.

In the narrow conning tower, Mohr strained at the periscope, his number one packed in beside him and the coxswain, with the "Weyer," the pocket-book of the world's warships. Mohr could see now that she was a cruiser—high bridge and slanted, tripod foremast—but which cruiser? The coxswain thumbed through the pages. " 'Great Britain—Cruisers: County Class—Dido Class—Dragon Class—.' Here, what about this? 'Dragon Class: H.M.S. *Delhi, Despatch, Dunedin* and *Durban.* . . . Two closely spaced funnels, slight rake, after funnel smaller: after fire control placed high, immediately in front of the mainmast, trawler bow.' That must be it."

Mohr glanced at the picture the coxswain held up to him and nodded. So she was a Dragon-Class cruiser—British, for once.

Mohr took another quick look through the periscope to check the calculations, ordered a slight change in the D.A., or aim-off, then: "Down periscope." to wait for just the right second to raise it again and immediately afterward, fire.

Meanwhile the men had been briefed over the broadcast-system. They were used to cruisers. On the previous patrol they had encountered a British cruiser, fired at her and missed. Two days before, the American, and now—third time, lucky?

Mohr waited for two minutes blind, so that in the bright, calm seas and perfect visibility, the U-boat should not be spotted, and then at the moment when the cruiser should be in the sights, lying beam-on across the U-boat's bows, he ordered: "Up periscope. Stand by, torpedo tubes."

All he could see at first was a confusion of water and spray, then as the sea passed astern the horizon came into the lens. The cruiser had vanished. . . .

It was so unexpected Mohr could not restrain a momentary shudder, as if he were in the presence of the supernatural. Then, sweeping the full circle, he saw her again, almost out of range, to port. After zigzagging regularly for forty minutes, the cruiser had decided to alter course.

Mohr wondered whether to surface and take up the pursuit, then realized it would be useless to pit himself against a cruiser's reserve of speed. It looked as though he had lost her for good: the range was now too great.

Or was it? Would it be worth sending a salvo after her, just in case? West-southwest, she was steering now. On a sudden impulse, Mohr shouted:

"Stand by, tubes one, three and four."

Enemy bearing, range, angle on the bow. (Report from bow compartment: "Tubes one, three and four ready for firing.") Now the figures for the torpedo-setting enemy course speed, D.A.: Number one, passing them down on the voice pipe. "Ready for firing."

The first torpedo left its tube, followed closely by the second and third. Immediately, the chief and the outside E.R.A. were flooding the auxiliary tanks to restore the trim. Then all waited in silence. Stopwatch in hand, the P.O. telegraphist timed the run:

"One minute."

Throughout the boat the men waited, tensed for the expected explosion. Nothing happened.

"Two minutes."

No sound. The run was already longer than normal. The men began to wonder. . . .

"Three minutes."

Some of them were shifting restlessly now, certain it was a waste of time to wait longer. Why didn't the Old Man take a look through the "pencil?" Perhaps that would convince him.

"Four minutes."

And still in the conning tower no one moved. The Commander was silent. No orders came. Could you believe it? Who'd ever heard of firing torpedoes at such a range? One good thing: they hadn't spent themselves yet, they were still running, you could see that from the way the seaman at the hydrophones looked up for a second and nodded his head. So there was still a chance.

"Four minutes, thirty seconds."

Well, after all—if the Old Man still took it seriously, a good shot, like him. And he *was* a good shot, an amazing shot, come to think of it. Throughout the boat, interest suddenly began to revive.

"Five minutes."

Ah, too late now. A waste of three good torpedoes, the first they'd fired on that patrol.

At last Mohr jerked himself out of the trance. "Up periscope." He pressed his forehead against the rubber buffer.

A second later he was catching his breath. "A HIT! She's hit under her bridge."

In the distance, he had seen a gigantic column of water rear up against the cruiser's side, spreading upward and outward, hesitating, then starting to fall. . . .

At that moment, a yellowy-brown cloud shot suddenly out of the ship, swelling in separate puffs and streamers to a mountainous size. The torpedo had exploded in the magazine.

Then, incredible but true, the second of the three torpedoes hit her, close by the after fire control.

Seconds later came the sound of the first explosion, faint at that distance, then, quite distinct and separate, the menacing roar of the exploding magazine.

Soon the great curtain of smoke hid all from view, then as a faint breeze wandered over the water the cruiser was seen again. Listing to starboard and with her rudder jammed hard to port, she was wheeling slowly, like some stricken bird before it plunges from the sky.

Thirty minutes later, the sea was bare again and H.M.S. *Dunedin* was no more. The torpedoes had taken five minutes and twenty-three seconds to reach her, and the range had been over three miles.

PART III

SPRING 1942 — MARCH 1943

The Battle Reviewed

THE MILCH COWS

IN THE early stages of the war, German U-boats had been refueled at sea by surface tankers, but these were steadily dwindling in numbers as the enemy hunted them down, and in the period September, 1940 to April, 1941 alone, five were destroyed of which one was over 10,000 tons. By Christmas, 1941, losses had become so serious that the use of surface tankers had to be discontinued and the provision of an alternative means of refueling U-boats at sea devised.

The answer was the supply submarine, popularly known as the Milch Cow. These Type XIV U-boats were of 1,688 tons, had a range of 12,300 miles and carried 720 tons of Diesel oil in addition to their own supplies. Ten were laid down in 1941 and the first came into use in the following year. Meeting the patrolling U-boats at a prearranged rendezvous, the Milch Cows could deliver fuel, torpedoes, ammunition, fresh food, drinking water and medical equipment, take off sick or wounded members of crews and supply replacements.

By far the largest number of operational U-boats employed during the war were of Type VII, 517 tons, with a limited range of 7,000 miles. But the distance from Lorient to Halifax, for example, is 2,500 miles and to New York 3,000 miles, and when operating in these areas, the Type VII boats had hardly reached their patrol billets when they were forced to return.

The Milch Cows removed this handicap and when sinkings

declined in American coastal waters and operations had to be carried further afield, thanks to them the Type VII boats were enabled to play their part.

Their effectiveness was increased by another development. In the summer of 1942 an improved German torpedo was introduced with a magnetic proximity fuse. Whereas formerly torpedoes had exploded on contact with the ship's side, this new type exploded beneath the hull, causing much greater damage. Now U-boats were able to destroy their targets with one torpedo instead of two or even three. For the Type VII U-boat particularly, which carried in all only eleven torpedoes, this meant a great increase in fighting power.

WATER WAGTAILS

Off the British Isles and the eastern seaboard of America the concentration of shipping had been comparatively simple to find. But when the U-boats were forced farther out into the Atlantic, their poor range of vision proved a serious handicap. When a group of boats were trying to intercept a convoy the difficulty could partially be overcome by some going ahead to act as scouts, but here also the inadequate vision obtainable from the low-lying bridge of a U-boat made it impossible to keep a close enough watch over a wide enough area.

Sometimes, a lookout would be raised in a bosun's chair attached to the periscope, but this entailed loss of speed in submerging and could be done only in areas where aircraft were unlikely to be encountered. The same disadvantage applies to the Water Wagtail (Bachstelze), a one-man observation kite which was towed behind the surfaced U-boat, and this contrivance was used only on rare occasions in the South Atlantic.

The fact was, of course, that the U-boats would continue to be hampered by their limited range of vision until aircraft were provided to carry out their reconnaissance for them. But that meant aircraft carriers and a powerful surface fleet to protect them—in other words, control of the seas. Admiral Dönitz had to be content with the solution within his power, namely to concentrate the U-boats in packs and direct their movement by wireless transmission until they succeeded in making contact with the enemy.

U-boats in the Indian Ocean

Though the use of wireless transmission was kept to the minimum while the U-boats were assembling, the enemy developed after a time a direction finder that could guide him to the source of their high-frequency transmissions, enabling him to re-route his convoys to avoid the wolf packs and attack them before they had deployed. Admiral Dönitz was forced to shift the weight of U-boat attacks to more distant areas where these difficulties would, at least for a time, be absent.

Accordingly, from June, 1942, the U-boats began to operate in strength in areas south of the Equator, appearing first off the Cape of Good Hope, then up the east coast of Africa in the Mozambique Channel (where the Allies had concentrated shipping for operations in Madagascar), then in the Gulf of Aden to intercept shipping emerging from the Red Sea and finally in the Indian Ocean, where at Penang the Japanese permitted the construction of a U-boat base.

These operations were intended in the first place to disperse the enemy's forces and by compelling him to extend the convoy system over further vast areas of ocean, slow down the whole worldwide movement of Allied seaborne supplies. Their secondary object was to ease the strain on the U-boats operating in the North Atlantic and to supplement the efforts of the Japanese submarines in attacks on Allied shipping. The latter were in no sense of the word combined operations, as joint planning with the Japanese naval command was neither possible nor desired.

Radar

Meanwhile, the turning point in the U-boat war had been reached. Since the late spring of 1942 U-boat commanders had been reporting a strange occurrence. While on the surface recharging their batteries at night they had been suddenly floodlit with pinpoint accuracy by the searchlight of a plane and bombed. The planes had clearly been aware of their exact position.

Before the explanation could be found, the number of boats destroyed in this manner on the outward and return journey through the Bay of Biscay had reached alarming proportions.

After unpleasant experiences with a new depth-charging device, the Hedgehog[1], then with Torpex, the new explosive,
the U-boats were now faced with an electronic direction-
finding transmitter small enough to be carried by aircraft.
Though radar was in itself nothing new—it had long been in
use on land, for example, against aircraft—the apparatus had
previously been too large and too heavy to be fitted even to
warships, except those above a certain size.

At first in Wellington bombers, then in Liberators and
Catalinas and finally in all very long-range aircraft, the enemy's 1½ meter A.S.V.[2], as it was called, was employed in
night patrols in the Bay of Biscay, covering the approaches to
the U-boat bases on the French Atlantic coast.

Hitherto the U-boats had been comparatively safe in these
areas at night or in bad visibility by day, but with A.S.V. the
enemy was no longer dependent on optical visibility and could
locate and destroy them at any moment throughout the
twenty-four hours.

Proceeding on the surface, the U-boat's Diesels would
drown the noise of the aircraft engines and the first intimation
of danger would be when the blinding glare of a searchlight
struck suddenly down, too late for the U-boat to dive or the
A.A. guns to be manned.

The Leigh Light would be switched on from a height of
about 150 feet only at the last moment, when it was calculated
to shine directly onto the U-boat. It was mounted in such a
way that the bomb sights came onto the target simultaneously.

Some relief was afforded to the U-boats by equipping them
with receivers that gave warning when they were in the
enemy's radar beam. At first, instruments of French manufacture were used, called Metox, which worked on the acoustical
principle. These were superseded in the autumn of 1942 by a

---

[1] The Hedgehog was a device for *throwing* depth charges, several
together, in a pattern. Previously they had been *dropped* from a
chute in the warship's stern. The advantage of the new method was
speed in getting the depth charges to the right place before Asdic
contact with the U-boat was lost.—*Translator.*

[2] A.S.V.=Aircraft to Surface Vessel. It was based on the same
principle as all radiolocating devices: a transmitter emitting a beam
of electromagnetic waves of very short length and at very high
frequency and receiving back the pulses reflected by the object
beamed.—*Translator.*

German apparatus, the FuMB, short for Funkmessbeobach-tungsgerät, or radar search-receiver.

Though the U-boats now received warning in time for them to avoid surprise attack and though the numbers actually sighted by Allied aircraft dropped from 120 in September to 57 in October, 1942, the fact remained that the U-boats were hardly less vulnerable submerged than surfaced, for once radar had revealed their exact position the enemy could summon reinforcements in the form of surface vessels or aircraft that forced the U-boat to remain submerged while they plastered the area with depth charges. As a result, even though they might succeed in making the initial contact with enemy merchant ships, the U-boats now had much greater difficulty in remaining undetected until they had delivered their attack.

In any case, what partial relief the German search-receiver did afford was not to last for long and early in 1943 Allied aircraft resumed their surprise attacks without the FuMB giving warning of their approach.

In their attempts to discover the reason, German scientists found that the FuMB emitted radiations and, believing that the enemy were taking advantage of the fact to locate the U-boats without having to employ their own radar, the Naval High Command forbade U-boats to use their search-receivers unless they had been proved free of radiations.

In fact, however, the surprise attacks were not due to the radiations of the German search-receiver—of which the Allies at that time were unaware—but to the new British centimeter-radar, called H_2S,[1] whose wave-length the FuMB could not record. Nevertheless, though the Germans in due course became aware of the existence of H_2S and took measures to combat it, they never realized until after the war that it had been the culprit all along.

Meanwhile various decoy devices were introduced on the German side to mislead the Allied 1½-meter A.S.V., for example, Aphrodite, which consisted of strips of tinfoil affixed to a balloon trailed in the wake of the U-boat. Another effective counter, this time to the Asdics, was the Bold, a cartridge fired from the stern of a submerged U-boat which produced

---

[1] H_2S=hydrogen sulphide, a gas smelling of bad eggs. Said to have been applied to the centimeter-radar after an eminent scientist had commented on the idea: "It stinks!"—*Translator.*

bubbles reflecting the waves of the Asdic in a way similar to the hull of a submarine.

THE ZENITH OF THE U-BOATS' SUCCESS

The last six months of 1942 marked the zenith of the U-boats' success. Starting in August, after the tonnage sunk off the American coast had begun to decline, Admiral Dönitz resumed a day-and-night offensive in the North and Mid-Atlantic, maintaining for four months a force of over one hundred U-boats at sea against the Allied convoys.

This was the heyday of the wolf packs. Pressing home their attacks with confidence and skill, they sank in this period over two million tons of shipping—a rate which was approximately the same as that achieved earlier in the year in the U-boat Paradise. In November, 1942, the monthly total of tonnage sunk by U-boats reached the highest of the whole war, 117 ships of over 700,000 tons. Of these, 72 ships were in convoy.

Nevertheless, these successes were deceptive, for behind the strikingly high figures of tonnage destroyed lay the sobering fact that with twenty new U-boats being commissioned each month and only half that figure being lost, the tonnage sunk per U-boat at sea represented a decrease on that previously achieved. And this was inevitable, for compared with the spring of 1942, the U-boats were now encountering much stiffer opposition. The British hydrophones and Asdics had been improved, also the explosive power of their depth charges, and above all, the offensive tactics of their anti-U-boat groups. Every time the U-boats introduced a variation in their methods, the enemy changed his tactics accordingly.

Fighting Patrols

11 MEN ALIVE

MID-ATLANTIC, July 12, 1944: 3:15 a.m. The S.S. *Port Hunter*, a British freight-carrying liner of 7,000 tons, is thrusting at a steady 10 knots through calm, lukewarm seas. Suddenly, a gleaming fountain spouts up amidships, against her side, the air shakes with a heavy explosion and immediately she heels to starboard and starts to settle down.

Less than a thousand yards away, a U-boat commander watches his prey, waiting for her to sink, but obstinately she refuses and after a while he opens fire with his 88-millimeter. The first shot is a direct hit high in the superstructure, but then one after another the shells strike into the liner's side at the waterline. From the solitary gun mounted in the stern, the fire is returned—and still the liner remains afloat.

The U-boat withdraws into the darkness, to come in to the attack again from a different angle, this time firing a few rounds only and then pausing so that the ship's gun crew cannot range on the flashes. At last, two hours from the time of first sighting, with more than a hundred rounds of 88-millimeter in her hull, the liner sinks. No SOS is made—perhaps her wireless was wrecked by the torpedo—and no boats are lowered. Stoically, firing to the last, she goes down with all hands. . . .

July 13—twelve o'clock, midday. Wind, north, northwest, Force 4. Sea—slight.

The U.201 under her commander, Kapitänleutnant Schnee, heads eastward toward the coast of Africa. On the bridge the watch is being changed. "Matrosenobergefreiter[1] Petzke reporting relieved as starboard after lookout." The first lieutenant replies briefly: "*Ja.*"

[1] Able seaman.

"Matrosenobergefreiter Pauli reporting for duty as starboard after lookout." The relief takes over and the first man goes below. "Good—keep your eyes peeled." Then the first lieutenant's relief arrives and he too disappears down the hatch.

The humdrum of daily routine has resumed. Someone mentions the encounter of last night. "A hundred rounds, the fellow took—tough nut! It didn't do him much good, though, did it?"

The men going off watch, from bridge, engine room, motor room and control room, wait, tired and hungry, for their dinner as the food is dished out separately for each mess by the cook and brought round by the duty messmen. Then while the latter wash up and stow away the crockery, they go to "Zizzing-Stations"—settle down in their bunks to sleep. Gradually conversation dwindles, until only the disc jockey is still awake, playing snatches of tunes. But no one is disturbed, on the contrary: when the men get their heads down, so as to be ready for their next watch, they like to have music.

In the somnolence of the after-dinner stand-easy, the Commander sits at his small tip-up desk entering last night's action in the war diary. Then he too will go to his bunk and "listen in to the mattress."

The helmsman in the conning tower passes on a message to the control room close by. The Commander can hear the words clearly, as you can hear everything in a U-boat from one compartment to the next when the watertight doors are open.

"To Commander: Masts in sight, bearing Green one-three-O."

Before the message can reach him, Schnee is on his feet seizing cap and binoculars, ducks, leg outstretched, through the circular bulkhead opening into the control room, clatters up the ladder in the conning tower and is out on the bridge: "Where—?"

The officer of the watch points to the starboard quarter.

A tanker, steering northeast, but zig-zagging so widely that on each leg the U-boat lies alternately on her port and starboard bow.

There is not much point in attacking submerged and Schnee waits, keeping in touch, until nightfall, when he can try on the surface. The first torpedo misses—at the last moment the target alters course. The second strikes home and at once the tanker bursts into roaring flame. As the burning oil starts to flood out over the sea, some of the crew jump overboard. Others try to lower boats. Those few that reach the water are pulled away for dear life, loaded to the gunwales, while from all sides swimmers thresh out toward them, trying desperately to catch hold before they are overcome by the flames.

The heat on the U-boat's bridge, nearly a mile away from the burning tanker, is so intense that she is forced to move farther off. Somewhere a bright moon is shining, but now as the flames swirl out over the sea a canopy of reeking smoke blacks out the moon and the stars.

For six hours the inferno continues, until with daylight the U-boat can return to the scene. There alone on the oil-smeared sea is a single lifeboat with a heap of blackened figures, terribly burned and some wounded, but still—miraculously—alive. They have managed to set a sail. . . .

The U.201 has one torpedo left. Schnee signals the B.d.U. asking permission to stay in this area where opportunities seem plentiful, rather than carry on as instructed to join the group of U-boats operating off the African coast.

Within two hours an answer is received and deciphered. Schnee must have been lucky, says the B.d.U.; the amount of traffic in his present area is too small for a U-boat operating alone to be likely to achieve much. He is to proceed at once at full speed to join the other boats, as originally ordered, to help them in reconnaissance.

So the U.201 returns to her original course, southeastward, across the Mid-Atlantic, shouldering her way through dark, silken seas. The ocean stretches far and wide, deserted in war as it is in peace, and the crew can look forward to cruising undisturbed for several days. Regulations for once can be relaxed and while the lookouts, dressed only in shorts, prop themselves against the bridge screen scanning the horizon, the Commander holds court in the Winter Garden, the circular A.A. gun platform behind the bridge. Though the seats are hard, at least there is plenty of air. Round him, chatting, stand a bunch of off-duty men taking their turn for a breather.

On the after casing, a couple of stalwarts are fishing for sharks, with a line and an empty tin as bait. The flash of the metal in the crystal-clear water attracts them and there are plenty about, some visible in every detail of their evil form, including those coveted trophies, the fins.

Meanwhile night has descended and a fresh group of men are sitting with the Commander on the narrow boards round the perimeter of the gun platform, a tiny center of life amid the vast Atlantic spaces beneath the glittering, tropical stars. The U-boat swells and sighs, respiring on the quiet seas, while now and then a faint breath of wind meanders up, hovers, and passes on.

At dawn the wind expires and the sea now spreads without a ripple like sheet-metal or a kind of asphalt beneath the blinding, incandescent sun. Inside the U-boat the thermometer registers over 120° F.

With the U-boat heading southeastward at high speed toward the rendezvous, the day passes, closing in a gorgeous symphony of color. Again night comes suddenly, treading on the heels of twilight, but it brings little relief. The air is damp and stifling, like a hot towel laid over the face, and the stir caused by the movement of the boat is largely canceled by a slight breeze which sprang up at dusk and now blows from directly astern.

The U-boat glides on, the hull so steady in the calm seas that apart from the throb of the Diesels the men on the bridge can feel no movement of any kind and stand there like marble charioteers, outlined against the softly glowing sky. It will be another two days at least before any shipping is encountered.

Cleaving the still water, the U-boat leaves an eerie, greenly gleaming trail of phosphorescence astern, while the shimmering bow wave spreads its broadening arrow on either side. These seem the only moving things in the misty, shapeless void in which the U-boat hovers, as though suspended between sky and sea merged, seamless, into one.

With the passage of the hull, pale sparks are stirred in the depths of the sea and one can look down through layer upon layer of water to where the last dull glimmer fades mysteriously away.

"Da!—Herr Obersteuermann!" a lookout suddenly exclaims, to the warrant coxswain standing on the bridge. The latter lifts his glasses in the direction indicated. Destroyers!

"Commander on the bridge." A pair of them right ahead their bow waves just visible bearing down on the U-boat. "Port five! Steady as you go."

Put the helm down a fraction only at first and perhaps they won't spot us. They're closing fast, though—800, 900 yards? Turning to starboard. Of course they've seen us, at the speed we're moving that great glittering wake is impossible to miss. Perhaps they caught us long ago, though, in the screen of one of those radar sets you hear about.

On the bridge now, Schnee sees at a glance that it is hopeless. No good trying to dive, she'd never get down in time, and on the surface there is not a chance of getting away with that telltale phosphorescence.

"Clear the bridge. Quick. Down you go." In a flash, the four men are through the hatch, pellmell, while Schnee stands tensed and ready to follow them, both hands gripping the bridge screen, his eyes never straying from the twin shadows carving their way across these last few hundred yards.

He stands as though hypnotized, while his brain desperately seeks a way out, refusing to accept the inevitable. So this is it, the end. All right, then, but don't dive—better on the surface.

"Hard a-starboard." Thrumming evenly, sublimely indifferent, the boat heels over in her headlong course.

One hundred and fifty yards to go. Seeing the U-boat turn, one of the destroyers veers slightly to port, making to ram her in the stern.

" 'Midships!"

"Hard a-port." Seventy-five yards before the razor-keen prow descends. Hardly has the bow of the U-boat started to swing than the enemy spots the movement and goes hard a-starboard.

Twenty-five yards. A wall of steel rears up . . . it strikes— Past!

But as she swings round, the destroyer's side scrapes along the U-boat's hull.

"Dive! Dive! Dive." At last! Not waiting for the destroyer to pass astern, Schnee jumps for the hatch, bolting the cover after him, while the air roars out through the vents, the tanks flood up and the U-boat sags, groping down toward the safety of the deep.

Made it! But only just. . . . Schnee suddenly feels dog-tired, weak in every limb. We're out of that one, at any rate, and by the time he can come round again—

The first depth charges explode when the U-boat is only

50 feet below the surface. But they are wide; the destroyer had gone too far before she could turn.

At 130 feet, come the next series—nine of them, farther off still. The remainder follow harmlessly when the boat has reached maximum depth. After two hours the destroyers abandon their efforts and the damage can be surveyed. It is slight and by next morning can easily be repaired.

July 19. The U.201 continues on her way to join the other boats off the African coast. At noon precisely a submarine is sighted ahead, the conning tower outlined above the horizon. Uncertain whether it is friend or enemy, Schnee alters course to port—the longer the presence of U-boats so far south can remain undetected, the better.

That same evening the patrol area is reached. For four whole days Schnee cruises slowly up and down, with his one remaining torpedo, hoping in vain to sight a target. Not a ship, not the faintest sign or smell of one can be found.

Then in the early hours of the twenty-fourth, as he is closing in toward Freetown, he sights smoke on the starboard bow (Bearing Green four-O) and soon after on Green six-nine, the masts of another ship making southward from the anchorage. The latter, he thinks, is probably a freighter being conducted through the mine fields and the smoke will be from the warship escorting her. He decides to keep in touch with the masts, try to get an accurate plot of the target's speed and attack in daylight.

The smoke grows gradually fainter till at noon it drops out of sight below the horizon. It looks as if the warship is returning to harbor on the completion of her task.

The freighter is heading northwest now, across the Atlantic, but as the off-shore haze thickens to a mist, she keeps disappearing from view and pursuit is becoming more difficult. She is zigzagging on some fantastically complicated system, impossible to discover and several times Schnee all but loses her for good, maintaining contact only by diving and listening for the sounds of her propellers on the hydrophones. He must wait till nightfall, he decides, before trying to reach an attacking position—at periscope depth and repeatedly submerging, like this, there is not the faintest chance.

The rest of the day is spent in dogged pursuit. It produces at least one tangible fact, despite the enemy's shifts and stratagems: she is sailing at 6½ knots, that much is sure, to within a matter of yards.

20.00 hours—8 P.M. She is lost again, and the U-boat has dived to pick up the trail. Now, beside her screws, the sounds of distant explosions are heard in the hydrophones—depth charges. (Who is getting it in the neck this time? Bleichrodt in the U.109? Merten in the U.58?)

Rising to periscope depth, Schnee alters course a little to come on to the H.E. bearing, then continues at high speed toward the prey. Not long now before it gets dark. But tonight there will be a full moon, probably without a cloud in the sky, and the visibility here is better usually at night than in the daytime.

As the darkness begins to fall Schnee surfaces again and goes to full speed, making the most of the brief interval before the moon is up. A strong breeze is blowing from the southeast, but the sea is slight with, close to land here, only a gentle swell.

Already the moon has lifted above the haze, sliding from an orange-red disk into a floodlight of brilliant silver. The U-boat surges on—"Action stations"—with 3,000 yards to go.

Schnee stands on the bridge, the glasses ringing his eyes. The freighter is coming up clearly now, more and more of her upperworks, soon the hull. Behind him and to one side, the I.W.O.[1], bending over the night sight. He will fire the torpedo.

Here she comes still blissfully unaware in the full flood of the moonlight. She is a warship—a corvette!

Too late to turn back now. At 2000 yards the U-boat would be spotted immediately as she lay, beam-on, silhouetted—a sitting target.

The U-boat drones on toward her formidable opponent blindly, like an enraged wasp, heading for her starboard flank. It is a question of luck. Can the boat get close enough to fire before being blown out of the water by the enemy's guns? She will have to get really close—850 yards, at the most—long-range shots are no good against fast, maneuverable warships.

"Permission to fire, sir?" and again: "Fire, sir? Shall I fire, sir?" The I.W.O. is beside himself with impatience. Feverishly as he watches the range closing, while the fear grows that this

[1] I. Wachoffizier=First Watch-Keeping Officer=First Lieutenant (Number One).

time he has over-bid his hand, Schnee hangs on for a few
moments yet. "No! Shut up, will you! No, I will tell you—not
yet."

We'll make sure first! With our last torpedo we've got to
knock him out—1,500 yards and still he's waltzing over the
sea at his steady 6½ knots, without a sign of spotting us.
Incredible! Corvettes are supposed to be U-chasers, aren't
they? He's doing his routine patrol off the anchorage, that's
what it is, listening for underwater sounds, straining at the
Asdics and the hydrophones, while we go straight for him on
the surface! Diesels roaring fit to wake the dead! Surely he
can hear *them*?

Closer still—1,300 yards. "Fire now, sir?"

"Wait, wait, *wait*! Quiet! Not yet!"

A thousand yards. "Fire now? Fire?"

"Man, I tell you *no!* Not *yet—hold it!*" Schnee hisses frenziedly between his teeth; both whispering as if the enemy
could hear.

Schnee slackens speed a little for this last stretch so that
the bow wave and the wake won't be quite so conspicuous in
the unwinking brilliance of the moon. Through the glasses he
can make out the heads on the enemy's bridge. No thought
seems to have crossed them yet of what impends. . . .

Nine hundred yards, and now almost jovial and uncon-
strained, Schnee speaks: "Right, fire away, then . . ."

Not moving from the night sight, the torpedo-officer gives:
"Stand by, tube four!"

Eight hundred. Schnee jerks out, "Now—!"

The torpedo streaks out from the tube toward the target,
with a trail of silver bubbles in its wake.

Now, realizing that in a matter of seconds the fate of one
of them, attacker or attacked, will be irrevocably sealed,
Schnee is suddenly appalled by the risk he is taking. Ordering
both engines to be stopped so as not to give the U-boat away
in these last crucial moments, he decides on the spur of the
moment to get out now while the going's good.

"Hard a-port—and *beat it!*" As he calls down the hatch to
the helmsman in the conning tower, he involuntarily turns,
anticipating the movement of the boat.

At last—and too late—there is a sudden stir on the warship's bridge. The corvette starts to turn and a split-second
later, the torpedo strikes her abaft the funnel.

A mighty, echoing roar, swelled by exploding depth charges, stowed, apparently on deck, and the ship is flung skyward, shattered into tiny pieces, while a billowing surge of smoke and flame rears up toward the stars.

"Donnerwetter—" Then fragments of metal start to rain down on the U-boat. In sixty seconds, His Majesty's Ship —— has vanished and the only sign that she ever existed are two corpses, rocked on the moonlit, tropical sea. . . .

Schnee feels suddenly cold with exhaustion. He stares blankly at the men on the U-boat's bridge, seeming not to recognize their faces. They look up, waiting for their Commander to speak. There is silence for a moment, then he jerks his head, as though shaking himself free: "So what? We're all right, aren't we? *We're* still alive!"

12 TACTICS

NINE U-BOATS, all that could reach the area in time, had been ordered to converge at once for an attack on a convoy bound for England on the short route from the Mediterranean. For communication purposes, they were to be known as Group Endrass.

As the senior and the most experienced commander in the Group, Kapitänleutnant Topp, in the U.552, considered himself the unofficial boss of the show and the fact that Endrass had been a close friend and had only recently lost his life on a similar enterprise made him all the more determined that it should be a success.

What information Admiral Dönitz could supply to his U-boats sounded encouraging. The convoy was believed to be weakly escorted, though it had continuous cover from its own ship-borne aircraft. It had passed through the Straits of Gibraltar on June 9, 1942 (the same day that the U.552 had left St. Nazaire). The signal continued:

CONVOY EXPECTED CONSIST 21 SHIPS (NAMED), TOTAL 70,000 G.R.T. TOTAL ESCORT, 5 OR 6 WARSHIPS, OF WHICH 4 CORVETTES. NO INFORMATION RE POSSIBILITY DESTROYERS. . . .

As the U.552 headed southeast to intercept, the weather was squally, sudden brief showers of rain alternating with

bright sun. Somewhere in the distance, thunder was growl-
ing. . . .

At noon on June 13, Topp picked up D/F signals from
two aircraft and reported them to the group and headquarters,
though he was by no means certain of his own position, having been unable to take a star sight for two days. But shortly
after 2:30 P.M., smoke was sighted and he established contact
with the convoy—the first of the group to do so. Once again
he reported, this time exact enemy course and position.

Contact was not difficult to maintain as some of the ships
were producing heavy smoke, but for some hours Topp was
prevented from closing in. The escort vessels were pushed far
out on the flanks making repeated reconnaissance sweeps.
Topp found it was all he could do to keep a sufficient distance
from them to avoid having to dive.

Sea and weather conditions were favorable to the attack;
good visibility, cloud, moderate swell, with wind and seas
increasing. Topp patiently awaited his chance. It came, later
in the day, when his contact report brought other U-boats to
the scene. Then some of the escort was diverted to the port
side of the convoy to engage them, and Topp was able to
creep up on starboard unobserved. Then again he bided his
time, waiting until nightfall before closing in to attack.

When darkness fell an unforeseen difficulty emerged. Due
to strong phosphorescence in the water, the U-boat left a
gleaming trail in her wake. It soon became clear also that in
one vital respect, Dönitz had been misinformed. Far from the
convoy being weakly escorted, the number of warships was
unusually large and they were being handled with skill.[1]

To suit these conditions, Topp decided to employ novel
tactics. It would be suicidal, obviously, to attempt to deal with
the merchant ships piecemeal, in a series of separate, individual attacks, as in the Night of the Long Knives in 1940,
nearly two years before. Those times were over. Now, as soon
as the balloon went up in this convoy, pandemonium would
be let loose—a hail of bullets, tracer, parachute flares, warships wheeling in all directions, pursing their prey with new
locating devices, unloading depth charges whenever their sus-

[1] The escort in fact consisted of H.M. Sloop *Stork* (Commander
F. S. Walker, D.S.O., R.N.) with H.M. Corvettes *Convolvulus*,
Gardenia and *Marigold.—Translator.*

picions were aroused. Even if the first attack was successful, the U-boat would have little chance of making another. The only hope would be to get out at maximum speed and try to break in through the destroyer screen again later, when things had quieted down. So Topp decided to make a single run-out only, fire the entire loading of five torpedoes in the quickest possible succession at the maximum number of targets and then clear out while the going was good.

Shortly before midnight the men of the U.552 went to action stations. The merchant ships themselves were barely visible, only their wake showed, gleaming faintly in the darkness. They were sailing in line in two, possibly three, columns and their skippers being apparently unaccustomed to convoy work kept falling out of station, thus unintentionally becoming much more elusive targets.

Topp sought out the largest group of ships he could find, maneuvered into position and sent four torpedoes after them at twenty-five second intervals. Seven minutes later, after turning through 180 degrees, he fired the fifth from the tube in the stern.

Despite a range of well over 3,000 yards, three of the five struck home. The first victim, a freighter of four-thousand-odd tons, heeled over and sank immediately, the second caught fire and the third, probably the largest ship in the convoy,[1] a tanker of five to six thousand tons, having been hit in the bows, was last seen, forecastle already awash and sinking fast.

Before the last torpedo could be fired, a fantastic firework display had broken out. Parachute flares shone out, flooding the scene with their icy brilliance, while from the multiplicity of lights, flashes and flares, the whole surface of the sea, crisscrossed by surging warships, was turned into a glittering carpet of color.

The fifth torpedo was still running when its target stopped, and as Topp made off at full speed he realized that it was bound to miss, passing ahead. He managed to escape undetected into the darkness, and half an hour later, the whole display breaking off as suddenly as it had begun, the familiar, reassuring sounds returned: the whisper of the water along the hull, the lash of spray against the conning tower and in a

---

[1] It was, in fact, *Pelayo,* carrying the commodore.—*Translator.*

wing of the bridge the hum of the ventilator fans, drawing in air.

An hour later, creeping in again on line of bearing, Topp sighted the dark shape of a vessel and began to move gingerly toward it. Suddenly it turned and he saw it was a destroyer. Pursued now and recognized, Topp turned sharply away and with main motors assisting the Diesels, went to maximum surface speed. Losing sight of him and apparently assuming he had submerged, the destroyer dropped a series of depth charges in his wake, then turned and disappeared. They exploded nearly a mile away.

Topp came upon the destroyer again stationed on the starboard flank of the convoy.

Nevertheless he decided to attack once more from this side and in the same manner as previously, seeking out a likely group of targets and then firing the torpedoes in quick succession, each with the same depth setting and gyro angle, from the slowly turning boat.

By the time he was ready to fire, it was 4:30 A.M.—an hour after sunrise. The first torpedo was aimed at two overlapping targets—and was a "circle-runner"; the second at another single target; the third, at two more ships, overlapping as they steamed in adjacent lines of the convoy, and a minute later, the fourth torpedo, from a comparatively fine angle, at yet another freighter.

As Topp turned the U-boat for the last shot from tube five, he sighted a destroyer, coming uncomfortably close.

Meanwhile the earlier shots were claiming their victims: numbers two, three and four had hit.

Once again the pyrotechnics began immediately after the first explosion, before the last torpedo had been fired, and once again the last shot went wide. The skipper of the target ship, had learned something, obviously, from the fate of his friends, for at the decisive moment, just before the torpedo was fired, he had altered speed and it passed him harmlessly by. After this second failure with the after tube, Topp decided not to attempt a stern shot, in future, in this form of attack.

Making off on the surface, Topp again disengaged without being seen and once out of the area floodlit by the enemy's flares was able to keep in touch with the convoy.

By a quarter to six the two remaining torpedoes had been

loaded into the tubes. Five minutes later—after complying with another U-boat's request for a wireless bearing—Topp closed in to attack. But the destroyers were ready for him, and as he approached from the east, with hull outlined against the brightening sky, he was spotted and soon after forced to withdraw.

06.10 hours.   Came in again. Again spotted by destroyers and, before the attack could be launched, forced to withdraw.

06.32 hours.   Came in again, in broad daylight. Spotted immediately by a destroyer, which closed at high speed to ram. Forced to submerge.

Topp now decided to change his tactics. At a safe distance from the convoy, he surfaced and made at full speed for a position on its probable line of advance. There he went to periscope depth and waited for the ships to come up with him. But meanwhile they had altered course and when they finally appeared—eleven of them, with a twelfth straggling astern—they were far away, out of range on the horizon. At periscope depth, it would have been impossible to catch up with them and Topp had to resign himself to letting them go.

Finally another straggler appeared, this time within range, a fishing trawler of about 500 tons, sailing in ballast. Probably a Q-ship, thought the U-Boat commander. He wasn't taking any chances and he let her go.

Waiting till the ships had passed out of sight, Topp surfaced again and continued to trail them. Though forced to submerge on several occasions by enemy aircraft, he succeeded in making contact again during the day, aided by reports from other U-boats.

But to get in among the merchant ships proved impossible; the warships took good care of that. They were operating with such precision that it took all the U-boat commander's skill and experience to evade them. On one occasion the U.552 was nearly caught. Having dived to avoid an approaching destroyer, Topp stayed below for a time until all seemed quiet and then, not far from the point where he had submerged, came to periscope depth in the hope of being able to proceed. There, not half a mile away, stopped and waiting for him as quiet as a mouse was the trim outline of the destroyer! Before he could reach a safe depth again, she was overhead, unloading her eggs but the U.552 was lucky to escape with moderate damage.

Topp had lost contact with the convoy, but it was a clear night with good visibility, and in the early hours of the morning the lookouts reported a blur of smoke to starboard. Topp hurried to the bridge—to find the convoy spread out before him.

At first he had difficulty in ascertaining the enemy's course and formation; the angle on the bow seemed to vary widely from ship to ship. Then he realized they were steering due north, coming up toward him in line abreast.

Topp continued to close on a parallel course. Suddenly he saw the ship nearest to him turn head-on, as though she had spotted the U-boat. But at a distance of over three miles it was surely impossible. Neverthless as a precaution he turned to port, while the ship began to draw rapidly closer. Then he saw she was a destroyer.[1] Suddenly a parachute flare burst directly overhead; the next moment the destroyer opened fire.

Submerging, Topp turned through 90 degrees, went for three minutes to maximum speed on the motors, then diving deeper as the destroyer's propellers could be heard racing up overhead, started to creep away at dead-slow, "silent" speed.

But the destroyer was creeping with them, her H.E. bearing constant on the hydrophones. That meant they were caught. . . .

Soon, she could be heard as she passed overhead. Eight shattering explosions followed in quick succession.

The U-boat reared and plunged, bulbs shot from their sockets and in the darkness, voices come from the compartments, reporting the damage. It was bad—but no leaks, yet.

A second ship arrived above. Both started the listening game: stop—listen—move on a little—stop again—and listen again—and move, while brooms seemed to sweep the hull.

Several times the ships were heard as they passed directly overhead. Then they moved away and the sounds vanished from the hydrophones.

A long time Topp waited, then he came up to just beneath the surface and raised the periscope a fraction. It was dark outside and there was nothing to be seen.

[1] Actually H.M. Corvette *Convolvulus*.—*Translator*.

Another forty minutes and: "Open the lower lid, stand by to surface." He was impatient to catch up with the convoy, but puzzled to know the reason why the pursuit had so suddenly been broken off.

"Surface." As soon as the hatch was clear Topp was scrambling up to the still-streaming bridge.

Three thousand yards away, stopped, beam-on, and waiting was the second destroyer.

Topp immediately gave the order to dive. When the U-boat had reached the welcoming depths, the destroyer was heard moving slowly overhead. Then she passed away to port and there was silence. After forty minutes Topp came to periscope depth but could see nothing in the lens. Another half hour and he surfaced. All clear.

The air above was thick with the reek of Diesel fuel; the cause was soon established. Those first shattering explosions had cracked open No. 4 ballast tank and Diesel fuel from the adjacent storage tanks had seeped out to the surface, leaving a great oily patch on the water. The destroyer must have taken the U-boat for destroyed.

The new engineer officer, Oberleutnant Sellhorn-Timm, immediately set to work, repairing the damage. Meanwhile, Topp signaled Headquarters: Pursued with depth charges while attempting attack convoy, and then the enemy's position when last sighted and the fact that the ships had been sailing in line abreast.

It was too late to re-establish contact that night, but before even the repairs had been completed Topp was under way again, setting a course on the same bearing where the enemy H.E. had last been heard on the hydrophones.

Sure enough, in the early hours of the twenty-first, smoke was sighted ahead. By then it was too light for a surface attack. Keeping his distance, Topp reported contact re-established and continued to trail the convoy.

Soon after came the signal: "Group Endrass: Break off pursuit. Topp, return St. Nazaire."

On June 22, after a patrol lasting only nine days, the U.552 had sunk five freighters and one tanker, and was back at base for much-needed repairs. Of the nine U-boats engaged, she had been the only one to achieve any success against the convoy; the rest had never got near it. Several of them had been destroyed.

13 THE AIRCRAFT CARRIER

This would be Kapitänleutnant Rosenbaum's eighth patrol, his last before being posted to command the new pocket-U-boat flotilla in the Black Sea. (It was there, two years later, that he met his tragic end in an air crash, like so many U-boat commanders surviving all the hazards of seagoing service only to lose his life ashore.) On his previous patrols, ranging from Greenland to Cyprus, he had achieved only moderate success. But this time who could say? Perhaps his luck would change. . . .

Not that he had reason to complain. It was simply that, so far, the good luck had only just sufficed to cancel out the bad. On her last patrol, for instance, when ferrying supplies to Tobruk, his boat, the U.73 (Type VII of 500 tons), had been surprised by a plane in shallow water and had her stern completely shattered by a bomb.

Then Fate had hastened to make amends. Not only was the U.73 able to surface and, once there, remain afloat, but, incredible as it sounds, she succeeded in making her way back —on the surface, because she couldn't submerge—across twelve hundred miles of enemy-infested sea, from Tobruk, on the shores of Africa, to La Spezia, 200 miles east of Marseilles.

Throughout the journey not one single aircraft was sighted. And yet no other U-boat commander could remember the time when, patrolling in any part of the Mediterranean, he had not been forced to dive for aircraft practically a dozen times a day! Who could blame them, then, if they thought they were seeing ghosts that afternoon at La Spezia when the U.73, her stern crumpled like chewed cigar, came limping in broad daylight into harbor, weeks after they had given her up for lost?

For many weeks more she lay in drydock while as far as was possible in the foreign shipyard the damage was repaired.

Of course, Admiral Kreisch, (in command of U-boat operations in the Mediterranean) was not going to leave valuable U-boat men kicking their heels around La Spezia, and before long most of the old hands had gone. It would take some time, the Commander could see, to work up what was left of his boat and her crew—the "old sledge," as they used to call her—to their former state of trim efficiency.

So when toward the end of July the order arrived that the U.73 was to be ready to sail in the late afternoon of August 4, the news came as a considerable shock.

According to Intelligence, however, large-scale Allied operations were about to break in the Mediterranean and Axis U-boats had to be ready in maximum numbers to meet them. A convoy was even now assembling at Gibraltar that was destined to be of the first importance. With Rommel at the gates of Alexandria, supplies and reinforcements were urgently needed by the defenders and the convoy was to attempt to deliver them, breaking straight through the Mediterranean. Large merchant ships and fleet units were being fetched from far and wide in preparation.[1]

August 4, 1942. Under the fierce noonday sun, the U.73 had just crossed the harbor basin at LaSpezia, from the dry-dock on the far side to the concrete pier by the arsenal, where she was to take on ammunition and victualling stores.

As soon as she was tied up, the work began. The new cook, a fair-haired kid who had been working in the kitchens at flotilla headquarters, darted to and fro with his stowing plan, supervising the distribution of the innumerable boxes, crates, sacks, tins, baskets and parcels passed down from hand to hand into the hull by the working party on the pier, while the new number one, Oberleutnant Deckert, sat perched on a crate, ticking off the items as they went over the side.

Meanwhile the U-boat herself was not yet ready for sea and German and Italian dockyard workers were still flitting about with inspection lamps and Meggers, checking and putting the finishing touches to the repairs.

On the fore casing, the boatswain and the boatswain's mate (P.O.s in charge of artillery) were filling the cartridge belts of the 20-millimeter quick-firing A.A. gun. The job had to be done carefully, or when the time came to fire there would be a stoppage.

[1] This was "Operation Pedestal," planned not for taking reinforcements to Egypt, but for the relief of Malta. The convoy comprised 32 destroyers, 7 cruisers, the battleships *Nelson* and *Rodney*, 4 aircraft carriers and 14 merchant ships of which 5 reached Malta with vital supplies for the garrison, sufficient to save the Island. —*Translator*.

Meanwhile, the Commander paced up and down on the pier, trying to look optimistic.

They got to sea on time, of course. As always, the impossible was achieved, and sailing past the narrow isthmus that runs southeast from La Spezia, past the twin lighthouses of Tino and Palmeria, the U.73 began that evening her eighth patrol.

Next day the Commander started maneuvering trials to test the boat for seaworthiness and to train the crew. Several defects came quickly to light. On diving deep, one of the exhaust cutouts sprang a leak. The D/F coil, it was found, had not been properly waterproofed where the connections passed through the hull, while the radio-location set failed to function at all. There was a leak in the main bilge pump, a bad leak in the attack periscope gland and, worst of all, a slipping clutch on the main drive from the Diesels.

Apart from these major defects, there were a large number of minor deficiencies—hand grips for the bunks, for instance; hooks to hold open the doors in the watertight bulkheads.

On the second day of patrol a further complication arose. Four of the crew came down with gastric trouble and high temperatures. Almost everyone on board was feeling some ill effects from the hot summer, as was usually the case among German troops, who would insist on keeping to the same heavy diet, completely unsuitable in the Mediterranean, to which they were accustomed at home. As a consequence jaundice, of the infectious, catarrhal type, and gastritis were complaints common enough in that area not to cause any special concern. But the cases in the U.73 seemed more serious and it might be that she would be forced to return to base.

Meanwhile Kapitänleutnant Rosenbaum continued to his patrol billet north of Algiers, anxious not to miss the chance at which Admiral Kreisch had hinted when he had briefed him a few days before in Rome.

It had been reported, said the Admiral, that a British aircraft carrier (name not yet known) was to join the Allied convoy sailing from Gibraltar with the object of warding off dive-bomber and U-boat attacks. If the carrier could be put out of action early on, before the merchant ships were within reach of shore-based air-cover, or if damage could be inflicted serious enough to keep her out of action for several months that, indeed, would be something worth while.

But Fate at the moment, did not seem to have selected Kapitänleutnant Rosenbaum for the prize. By the following day, August 6, a good third of the crew were down with enteritis. Rosenbaum continued to rehearse them in dealing with the typical situations encountered by a U-boat on offensive patrol.

On August 7, the U.73 reached her billet in the western Mediterranean. Remaining at periscope depth during daytime and coming up for a short while only after nightfall to recharge the batteries and renew the air, she kept watch for four days without sighting anything more than a tanker in the distance and, closer to, an unidentified submarine, which the Commander took to be a Dutch boat, or possibly Italian, returning to base from patrol.

By now most of the sick had recovered, except for one man who was thought to be a case of bacillary dysentery and had, as far as possible, to be isolated. The remainder had shaken down well and by dint of rigorous training were gaining in efficiency and self-confidence. Some of the technical defects in the boat had been put right, and Rosenbaum could feel that he would have a fairly reliable weapon in his hand when the time came to attack.

The time came sooner than he expected, on August 11. That morning the hydrophones picked up propeller noises approaching from the west and fifteen minutes later, as the U.73 was making toward them, the masts of a destroyer were seen through the periscope three miles away on the starboard bow. Almost at the same moment, on bearing Green four-O, an aircraft carrier appeared, looking in the distance like a giant match box floating on a pond.

As she came closer Rosenbaum could distinguish five destroyers and one smaller ship circling round her. The carrier was making a speed of 12 knots and zig-zagging with almost right-angle alterations, the range varying between three and five miles. In under thirty minutes the whole force had disappeared from view.

An hour later a destroyer came up at high speed and passed within a quarter of a mile of the U-boat. Rosenbaum thought for a moment he had been spotted but, keeping his nerve, hung on, reluctant to dive and lose visual contact.

As soon as the destroyer was a respectable distance astern, Rosenbaum raised the periscope again—higher, this time—

and made a careful sweep round the horizon. Covering a good sixth of his entire circle of vision, a dense forest of masts was approaching from the west—the convoy!

With only the masts to go by, Rosenbaum just had time to make a rough assessment of the enemy's strength before an escort vessel passed up from astern and forced him to lower the periscope. He had seen eight at least, possibly more huge cargo ships, the tall tripod mast and fire-control top of a heavy unit (battleship or battle-cruiser), two cruisers and about eight destroyers, besides a number of smaller vessels impossible to identify.

Ordering full speed on the main motors, Rosenbaum headed at periscope depth toward the enemy. As the range steadily closed, with the U-boat to seaward of the convoy, he could see that the aircraft carrier *Eagle* was the last ship in the starboard line. Lying between him and his target on the starboard wing was a screen of seven destroyers.

None of the carrier's planes seemed to be airborne and if she kept to her present course she would come right in the torpedo sights at close range. Going to half-speed on the motors, Rosenbaum steered to converge with the convoy. The first three ships of the destroyer screen passed right overhead, but the U-boat remained undetected.

Cautiously raising the periscope again, Rosenbaum could see the starboard line of the convoy approaching—a cruiser and behind her in echelon the *Eagle*, each with a covering destroyer.

Beyond them in the next line but still only 600 yards away a procession of huge cargo ships was crossing his field of vision, eight of them, headed by a 10,000-ton freight-carrying liner.

They were sitting targets; one spreading salvo would blow the lot sky-high—it was the chance of a lifetime. Rosenbaum was sorely tempted to take what was offered, rather than hold his fire in the hope of getting in a shot at the *Eagle*. But he decided to wait.

Sixty seconds later the whole carrier from stem to stern came into the lens. Turning slightly to port again, Rosenbaum started the attack. All torpedo tubes had long since been ready to fire, with torpedo settings provisionally adjusted. He planned to fire a spreading salvo of four, set to run at a depth of twenty feet, at a range of 500 yards. At the last moment, when he could see that at least some of them were bound to strike the target, he ordered a slight reduction in the angle of spread so that all four would have a chance to hit.

When all was ready there were a few moments of agonized waiting while the bows swung slowly toward the *Eagle* and the *Eagle* came up to cross them at right angles; then with a last check through the periscope, the Commander ordered: "Fire."

After the four torpedoes had left the tubes the initial tendency of the U-boat to break surface had been checked, and she was starting to dive steeply, aided by flooded bow tanks and all spare hands forward, when the four explosions were heard. She was still diving deep when there came a strange, creaking, cracking sound, a drawn-out, rending groan—two minutes only after the torpedoes had struck her, H.M. Aircraft Carrier *Eagle* was going down. . . .

It seemed too good to be true until, twelve minutes later, the hull of the U-boat was shaken by a deep-throated, rolling explosion, the unmistakable sound of the *Eagle's* boilers blowing up under water.

Only then did the first depth charges arrive—fifteen, at first, some distance away, then another six, followed by six more, followed by three; soon after, farther off still, two more, and then, another two. The pip and hiss of Asdics could now be heard without need of hydrophones all around the hull, but broken up probably by the strong density layers the waves failed to reveal the U-boat as she crept, barely moving, as deep as Rosenbaum dared to take her, 500 feet below the surface of the sea.

For three hours the U.73 stayed at that enormous depth creaking ominously, almost stationary, with all auxiliary machinery stopped and bilge pumps idle, while water leaked in through the defective exhaust cutout, the periscope gland, the mounting of the D/F coil, the outboard trunking, and its weight built up steadily in the bilges.

Every member of the crew not required to remain on duty was sent to his bunk to lie down, so consuming less oxygen, and ordered to breathe through a potash cartridge. Many of the men put on their escape suits. The atmosphere in the boat

---

[1] H.M.S. *Eagle* took ten minutes to sink and in that time almost the entire ship's company were saved, 67 officers and 652 men. —*Translator.*

was stifling—hot, humid and foul. The men were glistening
with sweat. But they knew there was no alternative, that it
would be fatal to move.

After three hours, no more depth charges having been
dropped, Rosenbaum came to periscope depth. The hydrophones had developed a fault and were out of action, so it
meant taking a chance. But the first, quick all-round sweep
told him that the enemy destroyers had gone, and just as well,
for he could see a broad streak of oil spreading out from the
U-boat's stern. That she had not been detected must have
been due to the sunken *Eagle,* whose oil still rainbowed a
wide area of the sea.

Surfacing then, while the oil leak was traced to a damaged
fuel tank and the latter pumped clear, Rosenbaum made his
first signal to Admiral Kreisch, the C.-in-C. U-boats (Mediterranean):

> CONVOY COMPRISED: BATTLESHIPS QUERY ONE—A/C CAR-
> RIERS ONE, NAME "EAGLE"—CRUISERS TWO—DESTROYERS
> FIFTEEN PLUS—FREIGHTERS NINE QUERY TEN—

then, course, position and time when last sighted, and the
signal ended:

> HIT "EAGLE" FOUR TORPEDOES 500 YARDS. SINKING NOISES
> CLEARLY HEARD. DEPTH CHARGED, NO DAMAGE.

At ten o'clock that same evening, the men of the U.73
heard the Deutscher Rundfunk broadcast a special bulletin
announcing the sinking by a German U-boat in the Mediterranean of the British aircraft carrier *Eagle.* Soon after, over
the W/T, signal after signal began to pour in, congratulating
the U.73 and her commander, Kapitänleutnant Helmut Rosenbaum, on their outstanding achievement.

There was no doubt about it, they'd hit the headlines this
time! And yet it had been so simple, easy almost, thought the
young Commander—he'd had wonderful luck.

That night, Rosenbaum wrote in his war diary:

> WHAT A DAY! ONE OF THOSE WHEN EVERYTHING SEEMS TO
> SUCCEED! THE DYSENTERY CASE HAS BEEN FORTY-EIGHT

HOURS WITHOUT A TEMPERATURE NOW; TURNED THE COR-
NER, AT LAST . . .

and that seemed to give him the greatest pleasure of all,
greater even, than that famous deed that was to earn him the
Knight's Cross of the Iron Cross, the deed that lay now,
strangely stale and lifeless, behind him, in the past.

14 CONVOY P.Q. 17

BY REINHART RECHE, formerly Commander of U.255.

NOTE:

On June 27, 1942, a convoy of 34 merchant ships escorted
by 6 destroyers and 11 smaller craft, with 4 cruisers and 3
destroyers in close support, left Iceland for Archangel with
200,000 tons of war supplies, the seventeenth Anglo-American
consignment since the first of the P.Q. convoys had sailed ten
months before.

Northeast from Iceland, P.Q. 17 was to cross 1,000 miles
of the Arctic Ocean, head due east, passing between Spitzbergen and Bear Island in the direction of the Barents Sea,
then, turning southward, make a wide sweep into Archangel
on the shores of the White Sea.

All P.Q. convoys at this time were encountering strong opposition, but in the case of P.Q. 17 the dangers were greatly
increased by the presence in northern Norway of the German
battleships *Tirpitz* and *von Scheer* and the cruiser *Hipper*.
Against the possibility that they might try to intercept, a
strong Anglo-American covering force was being held in tactical reserve, ready to attack them if they put to sea.

On July 1 the convoy was spotted from the air and thereafter continually shadowed. On July 2 it was discovered that
the *Tirpitz* had left Trondheim. On July 4 the convoy was
temporarily held up by pack ice as it passed between Spitzbergen and Bear Island.

But Bear Island was only ten hours' steaming distance from
Altafjord, on the northernmost tip of Norway, and there was
strong reason to believe that the German warships had refueled there that same day.

If they tried to intercept—and it seemed certain that they would—the Allied covering force would be unable to reach the convoy in time and, as the only chance of averting its destruction, the merchant ships were accordingly ordered to scatter. At the same time, as they would be powerless against the German battleships, the escorting cruisers were withdrawn to the west.

The German High Command decided not to risk their battle fleet and it returned to harbor; the merchant ships, unescorted and scattered singly over a wide area, were now defenseless against U-boat and air attack, and in the days that followed, 23 out of the 34 ships were sunk. The remaining 11 reached Archangel, delivering 70,000 of the original 200,-000 tons of precious supplies.

The following account of a U-boat's operations against P.Q. 17 is given by REINHART RECHE, then commanding U.255.—*Translator.*

THE ARCTIC was new to us in the U.255, and strange, and strange it remained for as long as we were there.

Admittedly, Kapitänleutnant Oesten, of the operations staff (Arctic) had gone through with us point by point the lengthy German Admiralty Instructions summarizing the lessons learned in two years of Arctic war, following up with a generous ration of his own good advice; admittedly, we had wintered in the Baltic, practicing navigation under ice and training generally for patrol in the frozen north, while the boat was fitted with heaters to stop the main vents, the transmitting gear and the periscope from freezing up; we had been reminded more than once of the difficulties of W/T communication in regions south of the Pole, but nevertheless the feeling never left us that we stood poised on the rim of the world.

Off Jan Mayen Island we bumped into a group of boats we had never seen before. Some of their commanders had been in the same entry together as midshipmen; all were old hands at Arctic patrols: Tex, Teichert, Marks, von der Esch, Zetzsche, Simon, and from the older age groups, La Baume, von Hymmen, Timm . . .

The sea up there was like silk, covered with a fluff of fog. Everything seemed intangible and mysterious. Strange birds followed the boat. The sun rarely broke through clearly enough to take a sight and if it did refractions distorted the horizon in a manner impossible to correct by navigation tables, or like as not the horizon itself would be blanketed in mist.

Everything in the Arctic was nebulous, including the movements of P.Q. 17, the convoy that was to take tanks and aircraft to Russia. There was said to be umpteen ships lying in Reykjavik, but the weather between Iceland, the Shetlands and Norway seldom gave German reconnaissance planes a chance to see what was going on.

It was toward the end of June, 1942, and the sun was continually above the horizon. One lost all feeling for time; only the regular changing of the watch and the succession of meals told how late or how early it was. But, even then—was it breakfast or supper you were eating? There would be no night attacks because—no night. And vision was never good for long; some kind of a shower would blot it out, usually snow. And those eternal curtains of fog!

From one of them, the dim shapes of two destroyers suddenly appeared and, after we had chased them for a while, vanished again. Then the W/T-snap reported first contact established with the convoy by some other U-boat—and immediately lost again. The convoy was thought to be heading in the direction of Bear Island, making a wide sweep round the north of Norway to avoid the German aircraft that were based there. But between Spitzbergen and Bear Island, the passage was believed to be blocked by pack ice.

We set off northeastward at high speed. Vision was no more than a mile, probably less. After some hours cruising at 16 knots, we dived to listen on the hydrophones; sounds can travel hundreds of miles underwater. We picked up H.E., clear and sharply defined, on a narrow band. So to the surface again, to give the news to the other boats; it might help them, *if* the bearings turned out to be right.

For another hour, we ran toward the estimated position of the convoy at 16 knots, closing at an acute angle to the H.E. to try to work round the flank. We were expecting to bump into something at any moment. Vision was continually changing, sometimes in a matter of seconds. The fog was rising off the sea like steam, forming into dun-colored undulating drifts.

Diving again to listen, we found the H.E. bearing had changed and we were relatively closer now to the source. It looked as though the convoy was making slight progress. Other boats were giving their estimations of its position, all different; it was too easy to fall off one's course in that soupy void.

But when we were only fourteen miles away, there was no longer any doubt; we were on the trail. Suddenly the fog started to lift and we were in a world of brightening blue.

As the last streaks trailed astern, there it was, the convoy, served up on a plate before us! Feverishly we started to count up the columns, then the escorts. Thirty-eight fat ships, bellies crammed with death and destruction for our boys on the eastern front.

We hurried out a contact signal, then made another, longer one, giving full details, starting with weather report, height of cloud base, etc., for our aircraft.

We kept right astern of the ships, in the fringe of the fog, so as not to be seen. The sea was like glass and the vision good—too good, if there had been an aircraft carrier with the convoy.

Out of the brown, woolly mass astern, a corvette suddenly appeared, belching black smoke, then, on the beam, a second. We went to full speed, but the one behind was slowly gaining on us. We hung on long as we could, wanting space to maneuver before we submerged, then dived. A couple of depth charges were dropped.

The escorts were having their work cut out shepherding the convoy and in those conditions it can't have been an easy job, holding a bunch of civilian skippers together. The British admiral was having his headaches, too!

It took us over a day to reach undetected a position twenty miles ahead of the escorts, where we could dive, marking time until they had passed ahead, and then surface to get at the worthwhile targets. It would take the merchant ships three hours to come up with us, but in that time the whole convoy might alter course in such a way that even at maximum submerged speed, we would never find it again.

And so it happened. Our first frontal approach found us some distance off the course of the convoy, within sight only of the leading destroyer in the port screen. It passed us close on the beam. A squint through the periscope revealed its masts rapidly dwindling and then nothing but the sun staring coldly into the lens.

The Commander cursing miserably, we shut the bow torpedo doors and set off again, eastward this time, after the vanished convoy. We must have been close to Bear Island. Thanks to the fog, we were able to stay on the surface: it was covered with a layer of thin, mushy ice. The echo sounder was climbing the scale alarmingly. Over the W/T we learned that our bombers and torpedo bombers were shortly to attack. Group Ice-Devil was also going ahead to intercept.

Cheering news, but still, to us in the U.255, the Arctic felt uncompanionable. At any moment, it seemed, we might fall off the earth into space. A seal surfaced and gazed at us curiously, then, with a neat dive, disappeared, to pop up comically again somewhere else.

Suddenly the sky was full of aircraft, all ours, heading northward. Then, a splatter of yellow-white puffs—the Ack-Ack—and then the shudder of bombs bursting in the Barents Sea.

Some hours later the torpedo bombers came speeding over the water, dipping their wings to us as they passed, while above them our three-engined Blohm-and-Voss reconnaissance plane cruised now, with its rhythmical, pulsing hum, guiding us to the convoy and insuring us an undisturbed passage.

Those friends in the air made us feel enormously strong, though now and again would come a blinding flash and watching with parched throats from the bridge we could see a plane blaze up in the sky, then, falling to the water, burn on as a funeral pyre. . . .

The Fox-Boat (from the emblem of a fox's mask on our conning tower) pressed on in the graying light toward the fighting. Outlined against the pale horizon, we could see the masts of sinking ships, with escorts standing by. The light conditions made it impossible to judge the range. We dived, covering the last stretch underwater, then came to periscope depth to get a better look; there was nothing to be seen. The air nearest to the surface had probably been chilled to such an extent by the melted ice that it reflected back the light like a mirror.

We surfaced, to find the masts were gone (sunk?) and the escorts were making off. Met another boat, U-Simon,[1] pressed on in company for a while. Then out of the fog a series of

---

[1] U-(Name of officer commanding).

red flashes and seconds later the sea ahead of us was flung
up by a 6-inch salvo. Turned sharply. Then the second salvo,
wider, this time. Underwater, we could hear the third, and
then propeller noises fading fast. . . .

Up again, to make wide sweeps, searching for the convoy.
Suddenly: "Commander on the bridge." Over on the horizon,
another fall of shot, but not a sign of the enemy. Yet the
vision at that moment was crystal-clear—odd. Then Harms,
our II W.O. and one-time deep-sea fisherman, recognized his
old friends—whales! A roar of laughter and relief on the
bridge, spreading to the men below. But was it so funny? If
whales could be seen blowing at that distance, then so could
we, blowing clouds of condensing exhaust.

Some hours later a single mast was sighted, looking uncan-
nily close-to and well defined. Plot and assessment gave a
speed of 12 knots. As we approached cautiously, a fat funnel
came into view, then the whole ship, 10,000 tons or more—a
choice morsel indeed. She looked like a fast ocean-sneaker,
dropped from the convoy to try to break through on her own
—steering for Nova Zembla, probably, giving a wide berth to
the Luftwaffe bases in northern Norway.

The W/T was bringing news of other lone ships attacked
and sunk by U-boats, at last, too, of the air-strike, which apparently had forced the convoy to scatter.

We closed in on our target, for a long time undetected—
we would have been seen long ago on the U-boat's bridge,
down to the last button, if she'd had a lookout in the crow's
nest—then at last she saw us and turned away.

Now she knew we were on her tracks we had to be ready
for all the dodges: sudden changes in course and speed, an
attempt even, if we ventured too far on the surface, to drop
back into the fog and come up again astern of us, before we
could make up our minds to dive.

We well and truly cursed the fog, the officers and I, and the
continually shifting vision, at the same time solemnly swearing, come what might not to let that steamer go; we would be
tough, wily and patient, like a true fox on the trail. . . .

At last, Fortune relented. After thirty hours of groping
through dense fog, we came out of it at last and turning south
lay in wait off the Matotschkin Straits. Sure enough there she
came rearing her fat funnel right into the Fox's jaws. . . .

Improved position slightly, then a textbook runout. We

couldn't miss, but to make sure, we gave her a salvo. Two explosions. She stopped, took on a list. Boats lowered. One more from the stern tube, to finish her off. She split open and sank. From a raft, with our scraps of English, we managed to get her name and tonnage: American ship *Alcoa Ranger*, 10,800 tons—some hors d'oeuvre!

The boats had red sails—we handed them bread and water and gave them a course for far-off Nova Zembla—they'd have a tough trip before they reached their "friends. . . ."

Victory mood in the U.255. We signaled Headquarters with a suggestion that the ships of the convoy had been told to try to reach Nova Zembla—we turned out to be right. Our long chase at high speed had brought us to the van of the scattered merchant ships hurrying to reach safety while their escorts were busy scrapping with other U-boats farther north and picking up survivors of ships sunk by the Luftwaffe.

Soon another pair of masts came out of the fog toward us, followed closely by two more. The traffic here was about as thick as that encountered earlier in the year off the American coast—the U-boat Paradise all over again, except that this one was rather colder. We had to fire at the first ship at an acute angle because the second was almost on top of us, and we missed. As a result, both got away. But we had no need to chase after them for at that moment a third conveniently put in an appearance to northward. This time the torpedo found its mark. Then we got up the ammunition, and the sailors were allowed to amuse themselves gunning her from the surface with the 88-millimeter. They left the good ship *Olopatra* a blazing wreck.

We were getting our hands in now, and soon after our cannon claimed another victim. The gun's crew were right in their element. Smothered with smoke and steam, another steamer went to the fishes.

By now the area must be getting a bad name, we felt, so we headed southwest to a position on the escape route to the White Sea, where Russian ice breakers had cleared the approaches to Archangel. One morning off the Kola Peninsula we saw a strange sight—two enemy merchant ships with an escort apparently sailing upside-down in the clouds, their inverted masts balanced on the tips of the real ones which at that moment were coming over the horizon! We wondered whether the outline of the U.255 was similarly stamped in the sky. Soon, in fact, the Russians did send a rickety biplane after us and we had to cover a good distance underwater before the perpetual daylight would allow us to escape at high speed toward the north.

Concluding U-boat operations against P.Q. 17, those boats not yet run out of fuel were ordered to comb certain areas of the route over which the convoy had passed so as to pick up any stragglers. We were allotted the northernmost sector, extending to north latitude 76°, then south to Bear Island and homeward via Andfjord to Narvik.

We came upon a Dutch ship, the *Paulus Potter,* stuck fast in pack ice and abandoned by her crew. She had been torpedoed from the air and her engine room was underwater. The crew had obviously left in a hurry—the breakfast was still on the table—and we found a deed box, stove in but with contents still intact, that no one had bothered to throw overboard. Among other useful information it contained the new signal book for convoys and a complete list of all the ships in the convoy. Thanks to our find the German High Command was able a few days later to announce the fate of the famous P.Q. 17 before even the enemy knew it himself.

PART IV

SPRING 1943 — MAY 1945

The Battle Reviewed

MOUNTING DIFFICULTIES

For some months in the spring and summer of 1942 German U-boat losses had increased alarmingly through the introduction of airborne A.S.V. Then a German radar search receiver had been developed and the losses had been confined for a while within tolerable limits.

We have seen how the U-boats continued their operations in the Atlantic with success, though sinking, in increasingly hazardous conditions, only a small proportion of the tonnage destroyed in the previous year.

The Allies were continually strengthening their convoy escorts and improving their equipment—destroyers, corvettes and aircraft in ever greater numbers, all fitted now with the latest and most efficient radar, Asdics and hydrophone gear. It became a considerable achievement for a U-boat even to get within range of a convoy.

Some U-boats had found their task assisted by tuning in to the wave length used for inter-convoy communication. One boat, for example, having picked up a signal from a destroyer: "Asdic not working," was able to attack and sink it without being molested. But only a few U-boats possessed wireless operators with sufficient knowledge of English to be able to follow this example.

Meanwhile, among the Allies the numbers of real specialists in anti-U-boat warfare were increasing and at the same time the improvement of anti-U-boat weapons continued. A new and potent method of firing depth charges was introduced,

spreading them out in a carpet to explode at varying depths.
Aircraft were supplied with specially constructed bombs.

The air cover for convoys and independent air reconnaissance now extended a net so wide and so fine that the U-boats
found it almost impossible to slip through. Areas which the
shore-based aircraft of coastal command were unable to reach
were patrolled by planes from escort carriers or from the so-
called M.A.C. ships.[1]

The convoys, both merchantmen and escorts, the independent naval support groups, the fleet air arm and the coastal
command were working together with masterly efficiency.
Equipped now with radar of greater range and accuracy they
harried the U-boats ceaselessly, almost from the moment that
they left their bases.

Few U-boats survived more than two or three patrols and
the dwindling numbers of experienced submariners had continually to be reposted to give seasoning to the new and untried crews. The latter had seldom time to shake down before
having to face the increased perils that all U-boats now encountered on patrol, and if a crew did manage to return safely
to base, all too often they had not a single success to redeem
the months of unrelenting strain. That was more damaging to
morale in the long run than the high casualty rate among the
U-boat men.

THE U-BOATS LOSE THE BATTLE OF THE ATLANTIC

In February, 1943, the new British centimeter-radar was
used for the first time by aircraft to locate the U-boats. The
German reaction has been described by the former Kapitän-
zur-See Giessler, wartime director of research in the communications department of the German naval command.

"The British 9-centimeter radar," he writes, "took us
completely by surprise, for German physicists had always
maintained that a wave length of under 20 centimeters was
unsuitable for use in an apparatus for pulse reflection. This
great and tragic error was destined to play a large part in
forcing Germany to her knees."

The U-boats found it almost impossible now, even in

[1] Merchant aircraft carriers.

massed attacks, to achieve success against the Atlantic convoys. On one occasion, 60 failed to score a single hit in attacks on one convoy. The following figures show clearly the severity of the crisis provoked by the new radar. In March, 1943, tonnage sunk by U-boats throughout the Atlantic Ocean was, in round figures, 515,000. In April, it had dropped to 240,000; in May, to 200,000 and in June it was 20,000. In the same months, the numbers of U-boats sunk, again only in the Atlantic, were 12, 14, 38 and 16—a total of 80.

This meant that for every two ships sunk, one U-boat was going to the bottom of the sea. Tonnage sunk per U-boat, which had been 100,000, according to Admiral Dönitz's calculations, was now reduced to 10,000—as he recognized and recorded in his war diary at the time, a disastrous trend.

Accordingly, Admiral Dönitz had no alternative but to withdraw temporarily all his U-boats from the North Atlantic.

This event was the turning point in the Battle of the Atlantic, a fact which was fully realized by the Allies at the time. Thus, in May, 1943, Admiral Sir Max Horton, said in a message to his command:

"The tide of the battle has been checked, if not turned, and the enemy is showing signs of strain in the face of the heavy attacks by our sea and air forces."

But elsewhere, in the South Atlantic and the Indian Ocean, the U-boats continued to sail fulfilling the unspectacular but vital task of forcing the Allies to devote large resources to the time-wasting convoy system and to maintain at full strength and efficiency their sea and air escorts.

So that U-boat operations could be resumed in the North Atlantic as soon as possible, Admiral Dönitz called upon his scientific advisers to evolve some means of combating the enemy's new microwave radar. It was not until August, 1943, that they succeeded in reconstructing a set and studying it in detail. The parts had been salvaged from two bombers shot down over Europe, the first near Rotterdam whence the set obtained its German name of Rotterdam Apparatus.

The new radar presented the German scientists with a serious problem. It could not be picked up by Metox or the German search receiver, for these had been designed to receive waves of the length employed in the earlier A.S.V. and they were therefore faced with the necessity of evolving an entirely new receiver in a field of radar which had for many years been neglected in Germany. The end of the war came before they were able to do so.

Meanwhile there remained the problem of giving the U-boats some protection against radar, either indirectly by strengthening their A.A. armament, so that when located by aircraft they could remain surfaced with some chance of survival, or by making it impossible for radar to detect them. The solution to the latter was represented by the Schnorchel, or Snort, and while this was being prepared the existing Types VII and IX U-boats were regunned.

Flak Traps

Apart from machine guns, the normal gun armament of a U-boat consisted of one 1-pounder A.A. gun on the conning tower and one 88-millimeter mounted on the fore casing. During the course of 1943, starting with the U-boats in the Mediterranean where the need was greatest, these guns were replaced by more effective automatic weapons, namely four 20-millimeter A.A. guns, mostly paired but in some cases mounted together, one of the excellent German-pattern 37-millimeter A.A. guns and the latest type of machine guns. To accommodate them, the superstructure of the conning tower was extended aft to include a low gun platform, while the conning tower itself was provided with light armor plating to afford protection against machine-gunning.

When sighted by aircraft, the U-boats were now expected to remain on the surface and shoot them down. At first, while the surprise lasted, the plan achieved some success, and in the late summer of 1943 the U-boats took heavy toll of the squadrons of the R.A.F. coastal command. But the enemy was quick to change his tactics. As soon as the pilot of an aircraft could see, from the men remaining on her bridge, that the U-boat was not going to submerge, he would fly off until reinforcements arrived and then return to attack in force. The U-boat command countered by sending the boats through the Bay of Biscay in groups and when this measure proved inadequate, turned some of them into flak traps, redoubling their armament in the hope that the enemy would take it as typical and treat all U-boats in future with a new respect.

The idea was not a success, as the following experience of a flak trap will show.

In July, 1943, on her second patrol the U.441 was sighted by a Beaufighter. Before attacking the pilot warily summoned two further Beaufighters, so that their fire power combined was no less than three 40-millimeters, twelve 20-millimeters and a dozen machine guns. Keeping out of range of the U-boat's fire, they proceeded to make a clean sweep of her superstructure, putting out of action every single A.A. gun, exploding two ammunition boxes and killing or severely wounding all twenty-four officers and men on the bridge and fore casing. Thanks to the fact that the aircraft carried no bombs and their cannon shells were unable to penetrate the hull, the U-boat was still able to submerge and finally, under the command of the ship's doctor, limp back to base.

This was one of the last experiments with a flak trap. Since the previous May some British aircraft had been fitted with a new rocket projectile which had sunk a U-boat on the very first occasion that it had been used. The introduction of the rocket made it too dangerous for a U-boat to stay on the surface and invite air attack, and in the autumn of the same year the U.441, together with other existing flak traps, was reconverted to normal use.

THE ACOUSTIC TORPEDO

For four months up to mid-September, 1943, the U-boats had not sunk a single ship in the North Atlantic. Then on September 19 they suddenly returned to the attack in this area, employing a new weapon, the acoustic torpedo.

This was the Zaunkönig (Wren), better known to English-speaking readers as the Gnat. Guiding itself toward the sounds of ships' propellers and machinery, it was intended for use against selected targets, especially warships. The Gnat was at first successful and in attacks on two convoys between September 19 and 22 was responsible for sinking three and severely damaging a fourth of the seventeen escorting vessels.

It was not long, however, before the British learned how to deal with this uncanny opponent. The early type acoustic torpedo was not sufficiently sensitive to pick up the sounds of a ship's auxiliary machinery and so, instead of making straight for the U-boat as soon as their radar or Asdics detected it, the enemy destroyers and corvettes now stopped their engines until they judged it safe to proceed.

Soon a more sensitive version of the Gnat was developed that could home on the noise made by ventilation fans, rotary converters and other auxiliary machinery. The British then countered with foxers in the form of squawker buoys, to lead the torpedoes astray. These had the disadvantage, however, of reducing the accuracy of the enemy's listening and locating gear, with the result that U-boats were able sometimes to remain undetected and attack successfully with an ordinary non-acoustic torpedo.

Nevertheless, the U-boats' comeback in the North Atlantic was not a success, a total of fourteen ships only being sunk in that area between September 19, 1943, and May 15, 1944.

The New U-boats are Planned

Meanwhile attention had been turned to the only permanent answer to radar, namely to evolving an entirely new type of U-boat capable of operating without loss of efficiency for long periods under water where the radar could not reach it. As a result, two electrically propelled boats (Types XXI and XXIII) were put into production and had reached the operational stage by the end of the war, while an entirely revolutionary type, called the Walter-Boat, powered by engines using high-test hydrogen peroxide, would have been ready for action by the autumn of 1945. These three types are discussed more fully in the next chapter.

The Snort

The air mast, or Schnorchel, as Dönitz called it, using a dialect word for nose, had already been fitted to some Dutch submarines before the war, but it had then been used solely for ventilation purposes. The Schnorchel fitted to German U-boats of types VII and IX was designed as well to supply air to the Diesel engines making it possible for the boats to recharge their batteries at periscope depth instead of only on the surface.

The Schnorchel consisted of two tubes, the first for air induction and the second, shorter and slightly thinner, for carrying away the exhaust gases from the engines. The tubes were raised and lowered together by hydraulic oil-pressure.

Before the introduction of the Schnorchel, U-boats had spent most of their patrols on the surface, diving only to carry out or avoid an attack. Now they were able to stay submerged for weeks on end. The record was sixty-six days; another Schnorchel boat stayed underwater for fifty-nine days.

But these were exceptional feats of endurance, for it was soon apparent that snorting made heavy demands on the U-boat crews and afforded by no means complete security against attack.

THE DISADVANTAGES

While a U-boat was snorting a careful watch had to be kept through the periscope to guard against surprise attack from the air, for though the top of the snort mast showed only as a pinpoint on the enemy's radar it was liable to visual spotting by the exhaust trail or by the disturbance which it made on passing through the water.

In other respects the crew had to be continually on the alert. In no more than slight seas the air inlet of the induction mast would repeatedly be flooded, and if the Diesels were not quickly stopped they would suck in air from the only alternative source, the hull, until with the reduced air pressure the men's eyes would bulge from their sockets. But some loss of air was inevitable, and after a time the continual variations in pressure would affect the health of everyone in the boat.

In the early days of the Snort, a further difficulty appeared. When the U-boat plunged deeply into the swell the exhaust would be unable to force its way out against the weight of water and would blow back into the hull. Often before the Diesels could be stopped the men in the engine room would have collapsed from the effects of carbon-monoxide poisoning.

A yet more serious disadvantage was the effect which prolonged snorting had on morale. At periscope depth, the U-boats were reduced to walking, or at best to cycling speed. Moreover they lacked an adequate field of vision; in daytime the area which could be seen through the periscope was minute compared with the vast expanses of sea which the enemy surface vessels could cover. At night, of course, the U-boats were completely blind, and now the Snort made them deaf as well.

When U-boats had recharged their batteries on the surface,

at least there had been lookouts with binoculars on the bridge; but now, recharging at periscope depth, the only means of keeping in touch with the outside world were the hydrophones, and the hydrophones were rendered useless by the roar of the Diesels. The cumulative effect of these restrictions was disastrous to a spirit of initiative.

Nevertheless, the Snort enabled the U-boats to remain at sea, for without it they would have had to surface at repeated intervals to recharge their batteries, and in the last year of the war, in face of the almost overwhelming combination of Allied radar, warships and aircraft, to surface spelled certain destruction. For the radar screen, in an aircraft flying at 9,750 feet, would reveal surfaced U-boats up to a distance of eighty miles, and though in high seas the range was less it enabled Allied planes to keep a constant watch over all areas where U-boats operated. The British coastal command alone was using 1,500 aircraft on anti-U-boat patrols, while the total of Allied planes so employed must have been more than twice that number.

In addition, there were now more than three hundred destroyers protecting the convoys and seven hundred escort vessels of other types—all these employed on the high seas. Engaged on inshore convoy protection and general anti-U-boat duties were a further two thousand ships. That it was necessary to assemble this vast array against the U-boats is an indication of the latter's achievement.

Against such forces, the Snort provided the U-boats of the existing Types VII and IX with much-needed security but with their slow submerged speeds, it could not restore to them the freedom which they had at one time enjoyed to pursue and attack enemy ships wherever encountered. When a target was sighted, it was no longer a question of attempting to outmaneuver the enemy so as to reach an attacking position, but simply of firing if he happened to be within range of the torpedo tubes.

These conditions offered little chance of success in the North Atlantic, and though a proportion of the U-boats continued to operate farther afield, the majority now returned to their hunting-grounds of 1940: the estuaries, channels and approaches round the British Isles. Here the Snort enabled them to lie in wait for their prey at the points where the heaviest concentrations of shipping were to be found.

Operating in British home waters, the Schnorchel boats were moderately successful at first, but their losses continued to be high. Of sixteen boats sent in June, 1944, to attack the invasion fleet in the English Channel, seven were lost on the outward journey, five more were damaged and forced to return to base and a further one out of the four that succeeded in reaching the operations area was later destroyed.

In 1945, in the Southwestern approaches and elsewhere off the British Isles, U-boat losses became heavier still: six in January, nine in February, fifteen in March, and again fifteen in April, while in this period the total Allied tonnage sunk in all areas averaged about 70,000 per month.

Thus it is clear that though the Snort had enabled the U-boats to remain at sea, it did not, as the German High Command had hoped, by any means restore to them their power of effective attack.

If the new U-boats had been ready in time, the whole situation would have been changed, no doubt to Germany's advantage. At any rate, the U-boat men, having survived undaunted this fourth and hardest phase of the war at sea, were looking forward to the chance in a fifth phase of regaining the upper hand.

Fighting Patrols

15 AT BAY

TILLESSEN had just finished a commanding officers' course at Gotenhafen on the handling of the ocean-going, Type IX-C U-boats when he received a telegram ordering him to report forthwith to the Tenth U-boat Flotilla at Lorient.

On arrival he was told he had been appointed to his first command, the U.516. That meant the Indian Ocean, probably, even Japan.

"Have you seen your command?" The flotilla leader's voice was coldly efficient.

"Yes, sir."

"Has she been passed by the dockyard?"

"Yes, sir."

"How soon can you sail for patrol?"

"Saturday, sir—three days' time."

The senior officer eyed him impassively. "No. You will sail for patrol on Friday, two days from now. You will muster your crew this afternoon, at 14.00 here, on the square. You will report to me tomorrow morning at 10.00 in this office, for briefing. Thank you." And the interview was at an end.

Put out by the O.C. flotilla's uncompromising tone and by the prospect of having to sail so soon after leaving Germany, Tillessen hesitated for a moment, wondering whether it would be worth trying to get the date postponed. Then, with a shrug, he turned and started to walk briskly down to the basin to find his new engineer.

The U.516 had just finished her routine overhaul after her last patrol. While she was in the dockyard some new equipment had been added: a radio-locating set, a radar search receiver, and some improved pattern Ack-Ack guns. The naval armaments office had clearly done their best, but with the present high efficiency of the enemy's anti-U-boat methods, a U-mariner's life was still not an acceptable insurance risk.

Moreover, two-thirds of the crew of the U.516 were entirely without experence and in the job of taking on stores they merely got in the way.

The old hands were full of gloomy foreboding. How, with these greenhorns on board, were they to get through the Bay of Biscay? Who was this new commander? What sort of a type was he—had *he* had any experience?

Yes, they'd need all their luck, the old stiffs reckoned, in getting through the Bay. The enemy pilots were quick on the trigger these days; since the spring they had been knocking off the U-boats like flies. But with only two days before the U.516 was due to sail the old hands did not have much leisure for brooding. The last few days before a U-boat sailed for patrol were fraught with danger of sabotage. The dockyard personnel at the French bases had acquired a very different attitude since 1940, thanks to unremitting British propaganda and pressure from the French Resistance. As a matter of routine, now, a German diver examined the pressure hull for sticky bombs before a U-boat put to sea. Once, in the U.516, on a previous occasion, a dead dog had been found in the drinking-water tank.

In such conditions, the presence of so many untrained men on board placed a heavy burden on the experienced members of the crew, but, in the case of the ocean-going, 740-ton U-boats, this was unavoidable. After a patrol lasting for as long as seven months a considerable number of the men would always leave the boat for promotion courses.

The new draft—lads of 16, 17 and 18—would arrive with the minimum of seagoing experience, those of the seamen branch with only their basic military training behind them. Those destined to specialize, would have had, in addition, a short technical course in their particular trade.

The Ack-Ack gunners would have been through a course in the use of their weapons, but not one would have fired a gun at night, and as U-boats had never been able to surface except at night since the summer of 1943, commanders and gunnery officers found themselves obliged, before sailing for patrol to hold practice shoots so that the new men could gain some idea of serving the gun and clearing stoppages in the dark.

In the majority of cases, the 16- to 18-year-olds would turn up brimful of tinsel ideals dinned into them by official propaganda. What life in a U-boat at war was really like they would not have the faintest idea. It would be weeks before any of them could get accustomed to the terrifyingly confined atmosphere in a U-boat—particularly at the start of a patrol, when it would be crammed full of stores.

And it was not merely a question of psychological adaptation. The stale, stink-laden air (quite beyond the powers of imagination to conceive), the lack of hygiene, the unwholesome food, half the normal adult requirement of sleep: such conditions were a mockery of those essential to life and it was only slowly and painfully that the human system could adapt itself to tolerate them.

On the day appointed the U.516 sailed for patrol to take part in operations in the Indian Ocean by a force of twelve Type IX supported by six Type XIV Supply U-boats. So that the force should not become separated all eighteen had to leave base at short intervals.

The length of time which they took to submerge made the supply boats particularly vulnerable to air attack and five of them were destroyed in the Bay of Biscay only a few days after leaving harbor. The sixth was lost later off South

America. As a result the operation had to be abandoned and
the twelve fighting boats allotted separate patrol areas. Of
these, two finally returned to base.

In September, 1943, when they had sailed, it had been common knowledge among U-boat officers that air attack could
be expected not only in the Bay and in coastal areas but
practically throughout the seven seas. The evening was the
most dangerous time, for then, as the enemy know only too
well, some U-boats would have to surface to check their position before the sun went down. The clinometer sextant, which
substituted an artificial horizon for the real one, was not introduced until the following year.

For the U.516, therefore, the early evening was the most
anxious part of the day. While the lookouts on the bridge were
searching the horizon for U-boat chasers, the chief responsibility would rest with the wireless personnel. Since the middle
of 1943, the Metox radar search receiver had been replaced
by the Naxos, a detector with valve amplifier and rotating
aerial of tuned dipoles, called Naxos fingers. As the aerial
rotated slowly through the full circle, a P.O. telegraphist
would stand by on the bridge, ready to hold it on the bearing
if a pickup was obtained.

The Naxos set was supposed to be sensitive to microwave
radar as well as to the earlier meter-wave-lengths, but as the
enemy's transmitting aerial would also be rotating and as the
dipoles had to lie exactly at right angles to the pulses in order
to pick them up, the latter would only be audible for fractions
of a second at a time and then, unless the dipoles were immediately stopped, only once. Hence it was necessary for an
operator to be continually on the bridge if the pickup was not
to be lost. Once the dipoles had been stopped on the bearing
of the transmission, the sounds could be held indefinitely and,
from the rate at which their bearing and volume changed, a
clear indication obtained as to whether they came from a ship
or an aircraft. If the volume was increasing rapidly, indicating
air-borne radar, the U-boat would immediately dive.

The radio-locating set with Braunscher valve supplied to the
U.516 quickly succumbed. The transformer burnt out and the
Mattress-type aerial collapsed under the water pressure and
short-circuited.

Meanwhile, making at full speed through the Bay at night
on the surface, the U-boat was entirely dependent on the

Naxos search receiver for obtaining warning of aircraft, the sounds of their engines being inaudible above the roar of the Diesels.

Soon radar pulses were picked up on the port bow, then another set, to starboard; then two more, on two further bearings. It is hard to convey the state of nerves to which this sense of being continually shadowed could reduce a U-boat commander.

Particularly to be feared were the so-called Economizers—aircraft which on locating a target slowed up the frequency of their radar pulses so that the search receiver in the U-boat would continue to pick them up at the same strength until the very moment when the bombdoors were opened. Even near misses, then, or machine-gun bullets could cause enough damage to force a U-boat to return to base. Many were only at sea for two or three days before they were back in harbor. Some U-boats tried up to six times to get through the Bay, returning after each attempt to the dockyard for repairs, before they finally succeeded.

Though the U-boat would be safe from air attack when submerged, a no less mortal peril awaited it underwater. As soon as it dived, the aircraft would call up destroyers, sloops or corvettes and these would then systematically comb the area with their radar. If they located the boat, a carpet of depth charges would descend. Or, if she dived too deep, they would bide their time in patience until, starved of amperes and oxygen, she would be compelled in the end to face her enemies on the surface.

If ships were not detected in the hydrophones within one or two hours of diving the U-boat would usually surface again. But the enemy's pilots knew the value of patience, and often the U-boat would no sooner have surfaced than it would have to submerge again. So it would go on, till at last the batteries would be exhausted. Then in desperation the boat would surface and man the Ack-Ack, with little enough prospects of success.

Many succumbed to these starvation tactics. In the spring of 1942, forty-eight hours after leaving Brest, Lorient or St. Nazaire, the U-boats would be clear of the Bay of Biscay and have reached the open waters of the Atlantic. Some of them, in 1941, succeeded in crossing the Bay on the surface in daylight. But in 1943 the same journey would take them anything up to seven days. Being compelled to stay submerged during daylight, they could make only slow speed for half the time, while at night, though they might stay surfaced, they would be forced by continual radar pickups to steer the most devious courses in order to avoid their pursuers.

After undergoing these tribulations the U.516 at last succeeded in crossing the Bay until she was level with the coast of Spain. Life then became comparatively peaceful after the tensions of the preceding days. Even the newcomers on board began to venture an occasional sniff at the fresh air coming down the conning tower, peering up at the disk of sky that showed through the open hatch at the stars, as they swung rhyhmically from side to side.

But many of these youngsters were still racked with seasickness and lay withdrawn and wretched on their bunks, longing only to die. Steeped in official propaganda, with its fairy tales of lusty, keen-eyed warriors leaping upon their enemies, they had never imagined that war could be like this. Now there was no escape; they were caught, imprisoned in that pestiferous dungeon, cheek-by-jowl with unfeeling, unpitying men, whose only thought, it seemed, was to press on implacably through the seas, farther and farther from home, instead of making as quickly as they could for the comfort and safety of land.

The poor lads were gripped by an agony of soul. If only they could get out—simply climb overboard and jump into the sea—instead of being shut in, battened down, in this deafening, reeking, reeling tube of steel. If only they had never volunteered. Their thoughts groped out toward home, far away, to their friends. They had no friends now. Shamefully they had been deceived, lured from their homes to meet a miserable and useless end.

As long as they were laid low with seasickness the youngsters were excused all duties on board, but for the rest there was plenty to do. After they had passed the Azores, the Commander and the engineer officer began a program of training. The first lieutenant and the gunnery officer took charge of the seamen, and the stokers trained separately under the engineer. Then the whole crew together were given battle practice; a shout, for example, would come from the bridge: "Aircraft action!" The boat would go to full speed, the helm be put hard over and the crews would man the Ack-Ack guns. Then suddenly the Commander would sing out: "Dive!" Everyone on the upper deck would make a dash for the conning tower —the hatch would crash down practically on top of them— clips pulled over—flooding valve levers down—and, tipping forward slightly, the boat would start to dive. At a shallow depth the first time, and then progressively deeper, the engineer officer would level her off, put on the trim and then she would go ahead slowly on the motors before surfacing again.

One night the U.516 was slicing her way through the Mid-Atlantic swell when a signal from Admiral Dönitz was received ordering the Commander to continue on toward the Panama Canal and giving him freedom of maneuver within a patrol area off Colon.

By then the boat had been at sea six weeks—in the early days of the war, the equivalent of a long patrol, but now in 1943 not long enough even to reach the patrol area. During that time the youngsters on board had begun to take some interest in their surroundings, accepting the U-boat more and more as the bounds within which a new life was to be found and feeling the need less and less to look beyond it to the world which they had left behind. There in that narrow space they found there was something worth doing after all, and as they were given duties to perform and entrusted with responsibility they forgot to rail against Fate.

Lifting gently in the seas, the U.516 thrust onward toward the southwest. In a few days she would be passing through the Dominica Channel into the Caribbean.

At night in that area it was possible to stay surfaced for eight to ten hours, and the stokers took it in turns, four at a time, to stand under the open conning-tower hatch and let the cool breeze play over their faces. They would envy the seamen on such occasions, the lookouts, searching far horizons beneath limitless skies. They themselves said good-by to the outside world the moment they stepped on board, and for months they would live with their machines, in dim artificial light, amid the universal reek of Diesel oil.

From 1943 onward the U-boat men began to feel not only isolated but excluded from the normal world. Wherever they appeared on the surface of the seven seas they would be harried and hunted to death. It gave them a currish mentality — Dachshund conscience as they called it—cringing, at the same time waiting only for a chance to snap back at their pursuers, to make them tremble before them. It was because they were feared that they were hunted and they took pride in the fact.

After the fifth week at sea all the fresh food on board had been finished, and thereafter the crew of the U.516 had to exist on canned foodstuffs: bread, potatoes, vegetables, butter, meat, eggs, ready-cooked meals—everything, in fact, had to come out of a tin.

Up to then there had been no complaints, but for some days now there had been a penetrating smell on board, different from the usual ones, coming, it seemed, from somewhere in the engine room. That was where the reserves of canned food were stacked, and when the smell turned to a stink and then to a stench it was time to investigate. It was decided to check every single tin on board. The work of stacking and unstacking proved more of a job than had been imagined but the result was a terrible discovery: half the entire stock of canned meat had gone bad and had to be ditched.

It was found that all the affected tins were of French manufacture. Immediately everyone thought of sabotage. "They reckoned we wouldn't get back," muttered the men. "They'd better watch out, though, when we do!"

They? The labels said simply: *"Fabriqué en France."* . . .

The U.516 spent a month in the Caribbean. Neither submerged by day nor surfaced at night did the faintest breath of wind come to relieve the well-nigh insupportable heat in the hull—140° F. The sweat streamed down incessantly, eating into the skin like acid and setting up painful rashes in the groin and between the fingers and thumbs. Contact with salt water became agony and fresh water was practically nonexistent.

Hair in that damp and broiling heat became a tangled, grease-sodden, dirt-caked mat, and beards were the same. The eyes were red-rimmed, bloodshot and smarted continually, while the nerves of the face and limbs twitched in uncontrolable spasms.

The men felt no better than they looked, and every spare moment they spent in a semi-coma on their bunks. Even when on duty they felt dazed, as though living in a twilight world.

Most of the crew had developed blisters, mainly on the arms and legs, and no treatment of any kind could persuade them to heal. Before any inflammation appeared the skin would become painful and then a few days later a crop of blisters would form, sometimes as many as eight or ten. After a while they would disappear of their own accord, leaving a bluish discoloration which would last for years.

During this period the U-boat was operating off the Panama Canal, and the deep water inshore enabled the Commander to creep in close to land during the daytime to watch for single ships making up the coast from Colon. At such times the strange life ashore could be clearly followed through the periscope; men going about their work, children playing, horses moving along the roads, cars flashing past. Even the fishermen could be seen as they worked from the beach, casting and hauling in their nets.

Any member of the crew who had a mind to could come to the periscope and help himself to an eyeful of land. But it was more a pain than a pleasure. For the U-boat men the glimpse of this peacetime world threw into relief their own pitiful lot, revealing it in all its bleak futility. Suddenly they would begin to hate the faces of the men around them, and everyone then would unload his spleen on his subordinate, picking on one and then another as the symbol of his deep and bitter disenchantment.

The Commander knew how they felt; it was hardly different with him. Lying exhausted on his bunk, he would wonder how long still that fetid, steaming swamp had to be endured before he could surface. For a while, by some aberration of mind, he could not bring himself to look at his watch; that, he told himself, would be disastrous. At last, his eyes strayed to the dial: seven hours to go, still, seven hours—seven—seven —hours. And he could feel his heart lurching like a leaky pump in that foul, exhausted air.

Then his mind turned to the thought of relief. Why should he not issue the potash cartridges, so that the men could breathe through them and the carbon dioxide be removed from the air? They were for emergency use only, still—

Better not, he decided; you never knew; they might really be needed some day.

In the summer of 1944 Oberleutnant Tillessen and the men of the U.516 sailed for their second patrol, this time to the Caribbean, off Aruba and Curaçao. It was not until they had

crossed the Atlantic and were nearing the area that they encountered any shipping. Then, off Windward Passage, a convoy was sighted sailing southeast toward Trinidad. It was
some hours before the U-boat could reach an attacking position, and by the time a salvo of two torpedoes had been fired
the ships were almost within sight of Curaçao.

Without waiting to see the result of the attack, Tillessen
went deep. Two minutes later came a single, huge explosion
and then breaking-up noises, the sounds that a ship makes
when it is sinking to the bottom of the sea. What it was that
produced that spectacular explosion and which ship in the
convoy had been hit have remained a mystery ever since.

But one thing was certain: at that stage of the war and in
that area where no U-boat had appeared for some time, the
U.516 could count on a wrathful and sustained pursuit. Surfacing again after some hours—it was at night—Tillessen
found the search receiver recording radar pulses from almost
every point on the compass. He dived immediately and tried
again a few hours later—with exactly the same result. He
realized then that there was nothing for it—he would have
to go deep and stay deep for as long as the air would last in
the hope that, by the time he was forced to surface, the
enemy would have given up the chase. The absolute maximum
it was considered possible to stay submerged was seventy-two
hours.

They started their ordeal in the U.516 with the thermometer standing at 104° F; at the end of the third day it had
reached 122° F. Even so, for the first forty-eight hours, the
men's minds would still function and their bodies do as they
were told, after that, they began to vegetate. Only the duty
watch remained sitting or standing, the rest of the crew lay
in their bunks, for in spite of chemical air-purifiers many
were by then showing signs of carbon-dioxide poisoning. No
sooner was the air breathed in than their lungs ejected it
again, their chests heaving as though under violent exercise.

Hour after hour on that terrible third day, while in the
world above a brilliant sun climbed up the sky, the crew of
the U.516 lay motionless, streaming with sweat, half-blinded
with agonizing pains in the head, silent and sinking deeper
and deeper into the mists of oblivion. Already, it seemed, the
seal of the tomb had been placed upon them, and where a
hand or a head chanced to lie, there it would remain until the

hull rusted and the sea broke in or the tide cast them up on the shore.

Then late in the afternoon of the third day a seaman came staggering from the control room toward the Commander's bunk, clutching at the framework to prevent himself from falling. He opened his mouth to deliver a message but no sound emerged. The Commander, too, was near the end of his strength and, in desperation he opened the door of a locker, hoping to find a trace of oxygen inside. When he turned again he saw the seaman had collapsed and was vomiting in a corner. With a gigantic effort the man raised a finger and pointed upward.

For a moment the gesture found no response in the Commander's brain, then the realization flickered across: that was what the man had been trying to say. He had come from the control room where the chronometer was pointing to eight o'clock—eight P.M. and time at last to surface. . . .

With a frantic effort of will, Tillessen hauled himself to his feet and groped his way toward the bulkhead. Reaching the opening, he got one leg through and then paused, suddenly assailed by an overriding desire to sink down and go to sleep sitting astride the gap. Then trembling with the exertion he managed to drag the other leg through and so came to the control room.

He saw the engineer officer, standing and actually able to speak. He said there were three men with enough strength left to help in surfacing, a seaman, the gunnery officer and the coxswain. With the Commander, the last two went gasping and clutching their way up the ladder into the conning tower while the engineer officer opened the valves on the blowing panel.

By then more than half the crew were unconscious and time was short, so without pausing to check through the periscope, without lookouts, engine-room staff, or duty watch, from 200 feet they brought the U-boat straight to the surface, to face whatever Fate might bring.

But first the upper conning-tower hatch had to be opened. The Commander tried, but he was exhausted. Dizzy and fainting with the effort, the other two then found a crowbar and managed to get it under the lip of the hatch cover. Then all three gave one last desperate heave.

Suddenly there was a deafening roar, and as though sledge-hammered, they were flung bodily backward against the periscope. For some seconds they were stunned, then they managed to clamber out on the bridge. It was not quite dark and the last bloom of daylight lay over the sea. It was deserted.

For fifteen minutes, on the bridge, they staggered about in a daze, gasping and retching as the fresh air burned in their lungs. Throughout that time the Commander gave no order of any kind. Then they heard the sound of the tanks being blown out and soon after came the familiar throb of the Diesels. Life had begun again. . . .

The U.516 stayed a month in the Caribbean, until all but four of the torpedoes had been expended and two of these being of the acoustic type, of which no one on board had any experience, the Commander decided it was time to start the long journey home. If he delayed any longer it would mean having to refuel at sea, for stocks of Diesel fuel were running low.

In the latter half of 1944 no U-boat commander would incur the ordeal of refueling if he could possibly avoid it. The last remaining supply U-boats had long since been sunk, and it meant that some young and inexperienced commander would be given the job of replenishing his colleague. But if either U-boat was to emerge intact, the whole operation called for considerable skill and experience. A rendezvous would be appointed for the two boats by headquarters and they would have to find their way to it, arriving at precisely the same spot at the same time, otherwise with the necessity of preserving wireless silence they would never meet at all.

Moreover, on a suspiciously large number of occasions, enemy aircraft had made their appearance at the very moment when the pipeline was stretched between the two boats and neither was able to dive, with the result that many U-boats had been destroyed in the act of refueling. All in all, therefore, it was not surprising if commanders avoided it like the plague.

So the U.516 was heading for home. Northeast of Aruba, while on her way, she sighted a tanker—a good 10,000 tons, but zigzagging with such large alterations that it was all the Commander could do to plot course and speed without losing her out of sight.

The tanker was running due south at 19 knots and with a

maximum surface speed in those waters of 15 (more in the North Atlantic, where it was colder) the U.516 would never have caught her if she had not been steering such a devious course. As it was, it took six hours to bring the torpedo tubes to bear.

The Commander fired only one, a T.5 acoustic torpedo, which, true to its type, headed toward the sounds made by the propellers and struck the tanker in the stern, wrecking her rudder. But, though out of control, she did not even catch fire, let alone explode, and it was realized then that she was sailing in ballast.

By that time they were close to the oil port of Aruba, and unless something was done quickly to send her to the bottom the tanker might be taken in tow and saved. Though she would have been certain to put out an SOS and warships would soon be on the scene, Tillessen decided to give her two more torpedoes.

Under their impact the tanker went down rapidly, and in a matter of minutes she had disappeared. Tillessen made off at full speed in order to get as far as possible from the scene before the hunt began and he was forced to submerge. In accordance with tradition the victory bottle had been passed round in the U.516 and, having so far escaped without damage, the crew were in high spirits. But none of the officers cherished the illusion that they would get away with it as easily as that, and sure enough in less than thirty minutes the hydrophones picked up propeller noises.

For the next twelve hours the U-boat stayed submerged, then surfaced again to charge the batteries. Hardly had she done so when an aircraft was suddenly heard roaring up, and the next moment, before the U-boat could dive, the bombs began to fall. The search receiver had given no indication of a radar pickup, but as it was a pitch-black night, she could not have been located, in fact, by any other means.

They were lucky to escape with near-misses which caused no more than a shaking. The following afternoon Tillessen surfaced again to complete the charge. Inside twenty minutes another plane was sighted as it started to dive out of the sun. The bombs exploded when the boat had only just submerged and this time severe damage was caused: two rents in the pressure hull, the worst one in the galley, starting a leak like a running tap, the other in the motor room: several cells of

the battery wrecked, resulting in a steadily sinking potential:
the trim regulator smashed: a high-pressure air-leak in the
after compartment and a high-pressure air group burst and
blowing off with an almighty roar in the control room.

Soon the battery went dead, and with the motors idle and
no steerage way the movement of the hydroplanes was of no
effect. Nevertheless the engineer officer managed to keep a
stopped trim by flooding and pumping alternately forward and
aft. All this had to be done by the light of pocket torches as
the main lighting had long since failed.

Throughout the night they worked repairing the damage,
bridging the gaps between the battery cells that were still intact so that they would be ready to go on charge. Toward
morning they surfaced again. Then, owing to leaks in the outboard blowing-valves, the boat started to sink slowly down
of her own accord, making it necessary to discontinue the
charge every ten minutes so that the Diesel could be connected to the air compressors.

After an hour or so of this came another air attack. Fortunately, the search receiver gave good warning so that the
boat was able to dive and avoid further damage.

The next time, they had been up for only forty-five minutes
when a series of explosions were heard about two miles away.
Then an aircraft searchlight struck down, revealing an enemy
destroyer!

This was too close for comfort, so, once more—"Dive!"

For the rest of that day the work went on, the crew living
entirely on dilute condensed milk. They had no stomach for
solid food and with the thermometer never below 100° F.
the exertion produced a raging thirst. As they worked they
took turns fanning each other with bits of cardboard; otherwise the foul air in that heat and humidity would have been
unendurable.

While working on the battery several men were overcome
by chlorine fumes and had to have absolute rest. All the time
the hydroplanes were picking up H.E. and occasionally depth
charges were dropped, though none in the immediate vicinity.

Meanwhile, being unable to move underwater until there
was juice in the battery and making only slow speeds on the
surface while one Diesel was putting in the charge, the U.516
was being carried dangerously close inshore. The charts
showed a strong tidal flow southward, whereas the boat would

have to head northward to make good her escape. On Christmas Eve, 1944, when the last charge was proceeding, shore
lights were sighted ahead. It was a terrible shock, until it was
realized that the tides had been carrying them northward, in
the opposite direction from that indicated on the charts, and
that the lights they were seeing came from the circle of islands
that marked the eastern boundary of the Caribbean. They
discovered, then, that it was only on the surface that the currents ran south; at two hundred feet—the depth at which
they had been lying—they had been taking the U-boat steadily
out toward the Atlantic.

It was a wonderful stroke of luck, for now the U.516 would
have to cover only a short distance underwater before reaching the compartive safety of the open seas.

And so it was that by the evening of Christmas Day the
U.516 had already left the Lesser Antilles behind and, with
her bows snuffling into the long Atlantic swell, was heading
eastward at last, toward home.

Each night, now, more of the familiar constellations appeared, Orion in place of the Southern Cross, Perseus, Capel-
la, and Cassiopeia and, soon, the Great Bear itself, peering
over the horizon. Clouds came up, the first they had seen for
weeks, shrouding the moon, while each night the wind sang
a higher note in the jumping wires. On the bridge, the lookouts would stand throughout their four hours' watch without
feeling the urge to speak, the sea imposing her silence upon
them.

The monotony of life in Mid-Atlantic was broken when in
response to the Commander's request a signal was received
from Admiral Dönitz giving position, date and time for the
U-boat to be refueled at sea. Together with another boat,
the U.129 (Harpe), which was returning from patrol in the
Gulf of Mexico, the U.516 was to be refueled and revictualled
by the U.544 (Mattke), which had just left base for the
Atlantic. The operation was to be carried out at a grid refer-
ence due west of the Azores.

From the earliest days of his service, starting with his ap-
pointment to the U.506 under Kapitänleutnant Würdemann,
Tillessen had kept a record of every single occurrence reported by U-boats in their wireless signals, entering the information on a chart kept specially for the purpose. Consult-

ing this now, Tillessen found that precisely the same rendez-vous had been given to three or more U-boats in the previous year and that they had been surprised by enemy aircraft with disastrous consequences. Was the whole process to be repeated now, he wondered, or had sufficient time elapsed for the enemy to have turned his attention elsewhere? There was no alternative but to wait and see.

Meanwhile, the whole operation of refueling had to be worked out in detail; the organization and navigational aspects by the Commander and the technical side by the engineer officer.

There were plenty of problems to resolve. In the earlier stages of the war, refueling had always been carried out in daylight, but, with the increasing strength and scope of enemy air patrols, this had become impossible and it was now always done at night. For the undertaking to be feasible at all, wind, weather and visibility would have to be exactly right. The pipe itself would be about the size of a firehose, with an inner-tube of rubber sealed into an outer cover of thick canvas. It would need constant watching, and so that it would not sink, life jackets would be spaced along it at intervals.

For two submarines to refuel in this manner in Mid-Atlantic was difficult enough in itself; when the whole operation had to be carried out under imminent threat of being attacked, it became a nightmare.

The final problem was of navigation; how to reach the exact position arranged for the rendezvous. No amount of care in taking sights or in dead reckoning could prevent errors creeping in, and, with the necessity of preserving wireless silence, U-boats had been known to spend days searching in vain for one another, often when separated by only a few miles.

In the case of this particular operation, therefore, all three boats were ordered by headquarters to surface two hours before sundown on the day concerned. This would give them about three hours of daylight in which to find one another and the added advantage of being able to complete their technical preparations before it got dark. Whether it held corresponding advantages for the enemy remained to be seen.

"Fall in the bridge watch! Duty lookouts in the conning tower!"

"Stand by to surface. Coxswain, the time, please?"

"Zero minus three, sir!"

Visibility good, sea 2 to 3, wind 3 to 4—excellent! Tillessen turned from the periscope for a moment as a message was passed from the hydrophone operator: "H.E., sir, propeller noises, closing Green, 0-four-0."

Better still; one of the other U-boats, surfaced already.

"Coxswain, the time, please?"

"One minute to go, sir!"

Tillessen turned to the periscope again for a final sweep all around. He saw a horrible sight: out of the misted sky, curving down like buzzards, came three bombers, aiming toward the sea about a mile away . . .

"Down periscope! Deep! Port twenty!"

"Flood Q!"—and, away to starboard, the depth charges dropped by the aircraft roared out—rolled—and roared and rolled again. . . .

The U.516 went to 200 feet, leveled out and started to creep away to port. Then came those noises that a ship makes when already beneath the surface, she sinks groaning and cracking to the bottom of the sea—breaking-up noises." A U-boat was breaking up and fifty men were dying with her.

For several minutes, in the U.516, no one could speak; here and there, a face muscle twitched; they stood as though turned to stone. Then they began to think of themselves again, and of their own chances of surviving the next few days.

Later that night, the W/T operator picked up a signal from U-Harpe to base. The U.544 had been destroyed—Mattke, who had been going to supply them with fuel.

A few hours later the headquarters signalled a fresh rendezvous for the U.516, north of the Azores this time in that notorious graveyard, Grid-Reference D. They were to be refueled and revictualled by Lauterbach-Emden, in the U.539. Both boats to surface only one hour before sunset.

At the time appointed Tillessen surfaced. He, his first lieutenant and three lookouts climbed out on to the bridge to find an enemy bomber cruising directly over their heads. "Dive!"—and away—

Absolved from the duty of reporting the sinking of U.544 by Harpe's signal, which contained the details required, the U.516 had not transmitted a word over the W/T for weeks.

Evidently U-boat commanders were right in their suspicions:
the enemy could and did decipher the signals transmitted by
Admiral Dönitz's Headquarters in Berlin. Official denials
that such a possibility even existed could not alter the fact
that time after time in the past three years, U-boats had
reached an appointed rendezvous to find that the enemy had
arrived there before them.

Two hours later, the U.516 surfaced again. Of Lauterbach-
Emden there was no sign. Tillessen proceeded to carry out
the drill prescribed for such occasions: thirty minutes cruising
at full speed on the surface in a wide circle, followed by thirty
minutes listening, submerged. By that means it was thought
that one U-boat would eventually hear the other. They did
not.

For two nights, as it later transpired, both U-boats continued this game. Tillessen was determined not to be the first
to break wireless silence and in due course he was able to
pick up the U.539's report to Berlin and the reply, giving
orders for a fresh attempt. That time they met and at least the
U.516 got enough fuel to last her to base, though the weather
closed in before she could fetch any food.

While the two U-boats were alongside each other Lauterbach-Emden had related that one set of propeller noises which
he had picked up while searching for the U.516 had turned
out to belong to an enemy destroyer; another to two enemy
ships, a destroyer and, some distance from the U-boat, an
aircraft carrier!

"Infuriating!" said the young Commander. "Just too far
away for me to get in a torpedo."

Tillessen grimaced. Yes, infuriating, of course, but—

He had a long patrol behind him and so had they all in
the U.516. Not so long ago a U-boat had met a terrible end
almost in front of their eyes. They had achieved some successes and they had no torpedoes left—and now they wanted
to go home.

16 SNORTING

"IT WAS an odd feeling" writes Karl Heinz Marbach, a former
U-boat commander, "to be sitting beside a lake in Bavaria,
on leave—dance music on the radio—drinking—an occasional
step or two oneself—good company—and suddenly to hear

your wife say: 'Hey! Listen! D'you hear what he's talking about?' "

"So you turn in your chair and listen, while a hoarse voice from the radio jabbers on about the Snort, giving the whole story, complete with details, accurate enough to make you feel: 'Curse that Allied propaganda from Calais.' "

" 'So that's the new gadget you're getting! Oh, yes, it is— I can tell by your face! That's what you've been holding from me! What sort of a thing is this 'Schnorchel,' anyway? Is it going to be any good? Come on—are we married, I should like to know, or aren't we?' "

A fortnight later—March 1944—back at base again in La Rochelle, I found I was curious to know more about it myself, to hear the chief's opinion of our latest acquisition. There seemed to be some snags attached to this Snort; of the first U-boats fitted with it, only one had returned—Mörle Schroeteler's boat—and he had been posted to a staff job. The others—no one knew where or why they had caught it.

But I said March '44: by then you had got used to coming off patrol to find some of the old faces missing, to hearing that "four boats from the Flotilla have failed to return," and you had acquired a robust kind of fatalism. Certainly you had ceased to find any point in wondering what sense there was in this eternal U-boating. Why worry? Wasn't it bad enough already to see every man-Jack of your crew return from leave more depressed than he went?

And the never-ending shop-talk in the officers' mess—you couldn't bear to listen to it now: ". . . trouble is, the U-boat's no longer a U-boat—that's where your trouble is . . ."; ". . . can't get a shot in on the surface, these days . . ." ". . . all I can say is, if you got within shooting distance of a convoy at periscope depth, then it was a pure and unadulterated fluke, that's all. . . ."

No. Going over the same old arguments—why, with or without the Snort, things weren't, couldn't, wouldn't be different. . . . All that was a waste of breath. When that topic came around again in headquarters mess, we got up in a body, my officers and I, and went ashore. As far as we were concerned, we'd made up our minds to invest in a Snort and that was that.

The men were all for it.

From our three previous patrols we had learned one useful lesson: the surface of the sea was no longer the place for a U-boat. If our newly fitted Snort could give us added hours submerged we would gladly put up with its disadvantages: that it had some was unfortunately no longer in doubt.

In the head of the Snort, for example, was a float valve, which shut automatically when seas came over, so that water would not come down the tube. It also, incidentally, stopped fresh air from getting to the Diesels, which then drew their supply from inside the boat. We would certainly have succumbed to claustrophobia, the first few times we experienced this, if we had not been accustomed by then to shortage of air. As it was, we were content, on the whole, to exchange this snag for the added protection which the Snort gave us against location from the air. We were grateful, and in our affection we christened our Snort Lohengrin, because it sailed through the water like a swan.

For the U-boats gradually assembling in western French bases for employment against the expected invasion, the code-name, Group Farmers, was chosen—and not a bad name for us, either, with our attitude of sly, slow-witted caution, our: "Wait and see—things could hardly be worse."

On our first trial with the Snort, the flotilla engineer in person accompanied us, so if things went wrong we wouldn't be the only ones to suffer. The thought was not entirely unpleasing; by then, the principle: "If I can't get away with it, then neither shall you" had long since become axiomatic in the U-boat Service. That's what happens, you see, when an instrument of war like a U-boat gets reduced from an aggressive to a defensive role.

With the flotilla engineer we went to periscope depth, trimmed, then raised Lohengrin to the surface. For the first time the Diesel was to be started when the U-boat was underwater. And start it did, but with a different sound to the one it usually made "Ah-ha—?" we thought, nodding sagely to each other in the control room. And there, already, stood the petty officer eyeing me reproachfully. Behind him the first clouds of Diesel exhaust were blueing up from the engine room. We'd met that one before, carbon monoxide poisoning —and it had left us drugged with sleep, powerless, like idiots, incapable of action. Without more ado we surfaced.

That it had been our own fault, that we had been nervous

and failed to carry out the proper drill, we had time to consider as a week later we were on our way to Brest to join Group Farmers. There we soon found another disadvantage of the Snort. The spray flung up behind it by the force of the exhaust made it very conspicuous in daylight, and that meant we would have to do our snorting at night and accept a further reduction in the already meager chances of attack.

One day in May 1944 the commander of the 1st U-boat Flotilla, Korvettenkapitän ("Crack-whip") Winter, called us together and expounded to us, Snorters and non-Snorters alike, the appreciation of the U-boat Command. A glance at the charts of the English Channel—depth nowhere over 50 fathoms—off Cherbourg, tide-rips up to 12 knots—coast on both sides with a narrow strip of water between—a warning that enemy air activity was "expected to be on a scale . . ." followed by every superlative that language could supply, and we had our motto for the invasion: "He who surfaces is sunk!"

But the operations order called, in words of moving simplicity, for a one-hundred-per-cent, all-out effort, abjuring us, if all else against the invasion fleet should fail, to ram, yes, even the smallest skiff.

A few days later, nine of us Snorters had our first operational exercise in the Channel. We took with us a de luxe assortment of torpedoes, the acoustic T5 Zaunkönig and the latest gadget, the Lut, for sheer complexity of handling, the Torpedo School's most successful effort to date. But we were more interested to see how Lohengrin would behave in the shallow waters of the Channel than in exploring the possibilities of these marvels.

In snorting, the official procedure was to use one shaft for recharging the battery and the other for going ahead at half speed on the electric motors. This method, we found, took almost as much out of the batteries as it put in and as a result the nine of us spent most of our time paddling like lame ducks around the Channel while our batteries were on a trickle charge.

In the U.953, after we had groaned and lurched our way past Ushant, we received a signal that some heavily damaged German destroyers were attempting to find refuge somewhere along the coast of Brittany and we were to be prepared, if necessary, to engage an enemy cruiser force pursuing them.

No sooner had the signal reached us than the enemy propeller noises were in the hydrophones, growing steadily
stronger and clearer. We surfaced, as instructed, in mid-
Channel at its western end. Our search receiver, mounted on
the bridge, was picking up continual radar pulses, from the
nearby English coast, probably, and from aircraft as well.

The operator had never heard anything like it:

"Just listen to this, sir—all over the scale—peep-peeping
away like mad."

By now it was midnight. Of the enemy cruisers there was
not a sign. At night hydrophones are often better locators
than a search receiver, so we decided to dive and listen for
H.E. The gauges were barely reading 100 feet, when overhead
came the roar of exploding bombs—just too late! We took
a deep breath and grinned sheepishly. Someone said: "I think
that will do for today. . . ."

Hours later the nine Snorters were signaled to return to
Brest. Lessons learned? That the present method of recharging the battery was unsatisfactory. One of the non-Snorters
raised another point. Too much of the pressure hull, he said,
broke surface when we were snorting and in time the result
would be a serious weakening of the structure: "Personally,
if I've got to get away from the surface, I'd rather hide my
boat behind a hedge than use that damned thing!" What could
we say—that we preferred to stay alive?

On June 6 the invasion began. Twenty-four hours later,
with the exception of the Snort boats, out of the group sent
to attack the invasion fleet there was hardly a single U-boat
that had not either been sunk or crippled beyond repair.

Meanwhile, we professional Snorters were busy with our
hundred-per-cent, all-out effort. It was found that while snorting the noise of the Diesels made it impossible to use the
hydrophones and someone had to sit continually at the periscope, watching out for enemy ships and aircraft.[1] Rather
than be blind as well as deaf, many commanders preferred to
stay at the periscope themselves throughout the whole time
they were snorting, but in our boat the view prevailed that
the commander should be free to make tactical decisions and

---

[1] Unlike British and American submarines, where the captain
stands at the periscope (in the control-room), in a U-boat, the
commander sat on a kind of saddle (in the upper section of the
conning-tower).—*Translator.*

with us, the two watchkeeping officers and the coxswain took turns at the periscope. The rest of the crew stayed closed-up at ramming stations.

Precisely off the northwesternmost tip of France, two days after leaving base, we found ourselves in the midst of a group of U-boat chasers. At first we saw only one destroyer with its reconnoitering aircraft, sailing outside the gyro angle for ordinary torpedoes. So number one suggested we practice the fire drill for our star couple, the Luts.[1]

Good. We were all in favor of making things fool-proof, otherwise it might be a case of the biter bit. Number one duly worked out and gave his orders for the torpedo settings, while in the control room below, the coxswain conscientiously checked them word for word with the instruction book. Then, just for luck, we fired the torpedoes off into the blue.

An hour later—we had long since dived and had our breakfast in peace—we had to repeat the exercise in earnest. The same destroyer was heard in the hydrophones coming head-on toward us, without zigzagging and very slowly. As it came it was making a horrible noise, like a circular saw slicing through wood. We had heard that sound before, during our practice with the Luts. With an angle on the bow of zero degrees, she was safe from normal torpedoes, but with acoustic? Easy. All too easy, we thought; there must be a catch in it somewhere. That sawing noise was probably to put our torpedoes off the track.

So I asked Number one: "In the trial run with the Luts, which side did you fire them?"—"Port bow"—"Then let's fire them to starboard this time. How far can they go before turning?"—"850 yards."—"Good; set them to 700."

Moving so slowly, the destroyer would have been certain to hear the torpedoes running in the hydrophones, but with foxers out on either side of her, she was deaf to all other sounds. Too bad that we hadn't fallen for them! One of the Lut salvo struck home. The other turned, and came straight back toward the U-boat! Just in case, we went deeper, so that it would pass overhead.

[1] Lut=Lagenunabhangige Torpedoes=Salvoes of independent torpedoes. These torpedoes, fired two at a time, could be set to run any distance up to 850 yards on straight, parallel courses, then to turn, each through any angle desired, before resuming a straight course to the limit of their range.—*Translator.*

Being curious to see what had happened to the destroyer, we came up to periscope depth again to find four more destroyers in sight, two of them making at full speed for the sinking position only 750 yards from the U-boat—and this time, without accompanying sawmill—just the thing for our acoustic fish.

We fired two, so quickly that the chief only heard one, then plunged below again. We were 150 feet below the surface, when all hell was let loose overhead. At a depth of 55 fathoms we laid her on the bottom and waited for what was to come.

Nothing came, for a while, until again that imaginary sawing of nonexistent wood began, 330 feet above us. Apart from a solitary Lut, which was not much good on its own, we had fired all the torpedoes in the tubes. The question now arose: did the sawing come from an acoustic torpedo foxer or from some kind of locating device? If the latter, then at 330 feet we might as well resign ourselves to our fate.

We pondered the question for ninety minutes—teacher giving us a clue at half-time in the shape of eleven depth charges dropped at random—then the air in the hull getting thicker every minute, we ventured up to periscope depth for a preliminary look-round. Destroyers miles away, almost out of sight!

We decided to reload the tubes. After that, the need for air became acute, so—up Lohengrin, if only for ten minutes to air the boat. With fish of both species in the tubes and fresh air filling out our lungs, we felt ready for anything.

Still in euphoric mood, we decided to let the chief try out the patent system he'd been thinking up for recharging the batteries: one Diesel with clutch out, entirely on charging, the other Diesel, clutch-in, propelling the boat and hooked on to the charge as well—result, no amps being taken out of the batteries at all.

Hitherto we had been afraid to try this method, for two reasons. The Diesel would drive the boat faster through the water than the electric motor and the strain might prove too great for the periscope, and, secondly, with both Diesels running instead of only one, the more violent changes of air pressure inside the hull might prove too much for our eardrums.

Our fears proved to be not unfounded. Each time a sea came over the top of the snort, the float-valve dropped, shutting off the air to the engines and in a flash, as they sucked

out the oxygen from the hull, we felt we had been lifted ten
thousand feet in the air. The moment the sea was past, then,
the air would come whistling down the snort again and in
the space of a few seconds, we would be back in the normal,
sea-level atmosphere at 15 pounds per square inch.

This new gymnastic so monopolized our interest that we
forgot all about the destroyers, until the coxswain at the periscope drew our attention to the fact that they were firing at
us with artillery! But they soon gave up trying to hit the head
of the snort mast, and Lohengrin went swanning on undisturbed until we had enough fresh air in the boat and sufficient
johnnies in the battery.

Whether our higher snorting speed had, in fact, upset it, or
whether, being a reconditioned one, it was due for a relapse
anyway, the fact remained that two days later our periscope
suddenly went on strike. Our home-handymen would not rest,
then, till—after extracting a covering dispensation from their
Commander—they had defied the most sacred of U-boat
standing orders and pulled it to pieces. They dried it, and then
they dried it all over again, but they couldn't persuade it to
work properly and in the end we were obliged to return to
base.

There followed for me a question-and-answer session with
the Admiral of U-boats (West). We were the first snorters to
have returned from near the invasion front. "Why is it, in
your opinion, that so far not a single U-boat has penetrated
the actual area of operations? Are the commanders afraid,
or is it, shall we say, that they don't like their comfort to be
disturbed? *Could* they—if they *wanted* to—?"

Staggering; I wondered what on earth I could say! Then I
remembered: at that stage of the war particularly, those who
achieved any success were in honor bound to defend those
others who had not. So I unpacked the whole works—the
Snort: its drawbacks and difficulties, ending with the suggestion that details of my engineer officer's technique for recharging the batteries should be signaled at once to all U-boats
at sea, as otherwise, if they continued to carry out the drill
prescribed, they would shortly run out of juice.

The atmosphere, at any rate, was now fully charged. Strong
words were exchanged—emotions ran high—the staff officers
(West) pulled peculiar faces.

We turned to the question of decorations; the question

turned to a problem. For previous patrols plus three destroyers sunk, I demanded ten Iron Crosses (First Class) for the
boat. Impossible, I was told, the men hadn't put in the re-
quisite days at sea. My entitlement was three. I protested.
More strong words. My protest was rejected. I protested
again. At last, the Admiral alloted me four—not for anything I had said, but because otherwise it would have meant
leaving out a P.O. who had been more days at sea than the
rest. That was the last straw: "I thought you gave decorations
for gallantry, not for globe-trotting."

Four days later we were at sea again. Crack-whip Winter
was consoling. He had recommended, he said, that I should
be put under arrest, but higher authority had decided to give
me one more chance of making good on patrol. Now
where—? Crack-whip had a bright idea: how about ferrying
ammunition to the surrounded garrison at Cherbourg? The
plan had been graciously approved.

In the end, it was a war correspondent who carried the can.
He had just got back in a damaged U-boat and wanted to try
his luck with us. "Is it first-hand experience you're looking
for," I asked, "or just somewhere to sleep?"—"Experience, of
course!"—"Is your eyesight in order?"—"Yes."—"Good,
then you can take your turn at keeping watch through the
periscope with two officers and the coxswain."

I never expected him, really, to take me seriously. I certainly never thought he'd be able to do it. But, in fact, he
turned out to be outstandingly good, and for four weeks our
guest took his turn at periscope watching to the satisfaction
of all, receiving his Iron Cross (First Class) in the general
hand-out at the end.

But that is to anticipate. When we set off for patrol, the
invasion fever was at its height and among the crew we had
nervous breakdowns galore. Admittedly the mass of secret
instructions we received before sailing in those days, all of
them "to be learned by heart," were enough to start anyone's
head spinning, but that was no excuse for developing psychological symptoms.

At any rate, I was not a little surprised when, soon after
leaving base, the second watch-keeping officer, who was also
wireless officer, told me he had clean forgotten the code-word
for setting the cipher key. That meant that we could neither
encipher nor decipher W/T messages—neither transmit nor

receive—neither be heard nor be spoken to by the outside world.

We couldn't return to base, in those days it would have looked too much like cowardice and in any case, after my private row with the admiral of U-boats it was unthinkable. So we tried to elicit the code-word from a passing U-boat: too strange a request altogether! They never deigned to reply.

For the whole of one night and the following day, then, the wireless officer tried to get at the answer by process of elimination, testing no less than six thousand of the more likely words to see if they would fit. While this was going on we lay off Brest, cruising slowly in a circle.

The following night, we determined to put out a call by the Hand Emergency Method in plain language. Ten times we tried, and got no answer. During the process, so as to show as little of the boat as possible, we surfaced at an angle, with only the forward section of the jumping wire with attached aerial and part of the superstructure above water.

The next night, getting desperate, we made five six-minute calls—transmitting for 1,800 seconds through air thick with enemy aircraft!—using the same method and telling the world of our misfortunes. It was incredible, but even that brought no result.

Half an hour later, when we were underwater again, the operator suddenly announced that he had been transmitting the whole time on the wrong frequency! So we tried once more for fifteen minutes, and at last, that time, got an answer. It was none too soon, for a few minutes later our position was floodlit by parachute flares dropped by aircraft. But by then we were no longer to be seen.

There was no disciplinary action: what point would there have been in charging a man with, one—youth; two—inexperience; three—having the invasion jitters? After our return from that patrol, the wireless officer confessed to me why he had forgotten the code-word. The morning we had sailed, he had learnt that his father had been arrested by the Gestapo and sent to a concentration camp. . . .

One outstanding feature of patrols in the English Channel was the unusually strong tidal flow. Snorting progress was so slow against the stream that whenever we encountered opposing currents, we laid the boat on the bottom and waited till the tide had changed. Another result of the tide rips was that normal mine-detecting methods proved ineffectual and to avoid the widespread enemy minefields in the Channel we had to rely entirely on the depth-sounding lead, the zeal of the crew, in particular of the coxswain, and the Commander's instinct. But it was a nerve-racking business.

About the second or third week of the patrol we came upon a large troop convoy and, soon after, a great cortege of supply-ships. Here the tidal currents came to our assistance, as they made the enemy's underwater locating devices inaccurate and, indeed, largely useless.

The relief was doubly welcome as the struggle to survive was proving an exhausting affair. To remain unobserved, it was necessary to snort only at night and then only for a few hours each time. The fresh air so obtained had to last us then for the following twenty-four hours. Once in that period only could we enjoy hot drinks or food, again, when we were snorting. Cooking, eating, drinking, moving about, even sitting instead of lying down, consumed too much oxygen. "All hands to their bunks" was a routine order with us for as long as we were at sea.

We spent so much time on our backs that our leg muscles became soft and we all began to suffer from pains in the back. I have never seen men do voluntary exercises (knee-bends, deep breathing, etc.) with such enthusiasm as the crew on that patrol, during the few hours when we were snorting and fresh air was free.

The carbon-dioxide content of the air in the hull, which was supposed not to exceed 3.5 per cent, used often to reach a point on the analyzer-scale that should long ago, according to medical opinion, have proved fatal to us all.

Snorting in anything like a sea was a fantastic experience. It would be damp and freezingly cold in the boat owing to the continual gale that was blowing through, and our ears would be strained almost to bursting with the incessant variations in pressure. On top of that, there was nothing but canned food and, of course, never a glimpse of daylight. All in all, we were not far, at times, from that unenviable condition—caneurosis.[1]

---

[1] In German Blechkrankheit, or Blechkoller, literally, tin disease, a wartime expression for a state of violent hysteria, induced, in the case of U-boat crews, by prolonged nervous strain coupled with the unnatural conditions in which they lived.—Translator.

But at last the four weeks' patrol came to an end. Two days before we reached harbor, the W/T operator brought me his log in which he had just entered a signal announcing the attempt on Hitler's life in the July Plot. There was not enough to go on to make any sense out of it and, anyway, all we cared about at that time, was that the toughest patrol we had ever experienced would soon be at an end.

A month is a long time to spend under water and when we had got safely back, we began to realize it. On an average, every man in the boat had lost twenty pounds in weight. But we had survived and an imposing reception committee was assembled at the quayside to welcome us.

So it lay, now, behind us: my private showdown with the Admiral, the forgotten code word, the July Plot—the patrol. Soon the Admiral himself would be beaming on us, saying how fit we all looked. Soon the medals would descend. Congratulations, even from Crack-whip Winter, would rain from all sides upon us. Such is War.

German U-Boats in the Far East

AUGUST 1943—MAY 1945

THROUGHOUT the war, the German Naval Command made strenuous efforts to strike wherever possible at the enemy's lines of communication at sea, and, even before Pearl Harbor, commerce raiders and auxiliary cruisers had already made the farthest oceans unsafe for Allied shipping. With Japan in the war it became possible for U-boat operations to be similarly extended, and, after the Japanese tide had engulfed, within the space of a few short months, Burma, Siam, Indonesia and most of the islands of strategic importance in the eastern Pacific, Germany approached the Japanese government with a view to discussing the necessary arrangements.

It was not, however, until early in 1943, when the Japanese were beginning to come under increasing pressure from Anglo-American naval forces, that they agreed to the employment of German U-boats in the Far East.

In May, 1943, the first four U-boats[1] to be sent to the Far East took on fuel and supplies from the *Charlotte Schliemann* at a rendezvous southeast of Madagascar and then proceeded to Penang, where they became known as the Monsoon Group. The first to arrive was the U.178 in the following August. A fifth boat, of Type IXC, finally reached Japan as a gift to the Japanese government.

Later in 1943 and 1944 the transport of raw materials between Germany and Japan was taken over by U-boats, the last group of surface ships to attempt to run the blockade leaving the Pacific in the autumn of 1943. Of these only one the *Osorno,* succeeded in reaching the West coast of France with her 8,000-ton cargo.

The German U-boat bases in the Far East were largely self-supporting, and the German staff had to struggle continually against the opposition of the lower Japanese officialdom. Most of the latter were men of peasant origin, rooted in the ideas and customs of their island country. Only among the senior officers and officials who were descended from the ancient Samurai could the necessary understanding be found to bridge the gulf between European and Oriental conceptions and ways of thought.

Thus the Germans were left to shift for themselves. They acquired the great 4,400-acre plantation of Tjikopee and, cultivating it with the assistance of Japanese workers, grew the vegetables which are so necessary to the comfort of German stomachs. They made a variety of preserved foods, including bread, which were packed and sealed in containers of pure tin. These were then loaded on to the U-boats returning to Germany, so providing food for the crew and a valuable raw material for German industry.

In all, during the war, 41 (36 German, 5 Italian) U-boats operated in the Far East. Of these, 30 were destroyed by enemy action, 5 were taken over by the Japanese, 2 fell into Allied hands on their way back to Germany and 4 finally reached home. The highest number on patrol at any one time in the Far East was 11.

As against the high proportions of U-boats destroyed in the Indian and Pacific Oceans, sinkings claimed by U-boats amounted to 149 ships of 925,042 gross register tons.

[1] The U.177, U.178, U.181 and U.198, all of Type IX (740 tons).—*Translator.*

Technical Developments

MAY 1945

It will be appropriate to mention here the technical projects in varying stages of completion in May, 1945, which, if military defeat had not supervened, might have enabled Germany to enter upon a fifth phase of the U-boat war with some prospects of success.

The Walter-boat

The engines of the Walter-boat, named after its inventor, consisted of gas turbines driven by a new type of fuel of which the main constituent was high-strength (80 per cent) hydrogen-peroxide.

A 600-ton U-boat fitted with these engines could reach a submerged speed of 24 knots with a fuel capacity enabling it to maintain this speed for six hours. Besides the main engines, the Walter-boat carried one electric motor as an alternative means of underwater propulsion, one Diesel engine to be used, if required, on the surface for driving the motor as a dynamo to recharge the batteries and, as the boat had only one propeller shaft, a further low-power electric motor for very slow, noiseless running when submerged.[1] Finally, there was a second separate Diesel-powered generating plant as an alternative emergency means of recharging the batteries.

[1] Submarines usually have two propeller shafts with one Diesel engine and one electric motor coupled by means of clutches to each. Normally the motors are connected in parallel, but for very slow speeds they are run in series, so that the voltage and hence, their output will be reduced. With only one motor, speed could not be reduced without inserting a resistance in the circuit and so wasting current. To avoid this, the second motor, of lower horse-power was provided.—*Translator.*

157

TYPES XXI AND XXIII

Production and Trials

Meanwhile, during 1943, two other new designs, the Type XXI, 1,500-ton U-boat, and the 200-ton Type XXIII, had been developed. As time was short, the prototype tests were dispensed with and, in December, they were put straight into production from the drawing-board.

They were prefabricated in sections by small firms all over Germany, and all that remained to be done in the shipyard proper was to weld these sections together—a process hitherto deemed impossible in shipbuilding.

Large numbers were to be ready for operations by the spring of 1944 but owing to Allied bombing and the destruction of important factories the delivery date had to be postponed until the late autumn of that year. Then surprisingly enough they were forthcoming in the numbers originally scheduled.

Thereafter they were delivered at the rate of thirty a month, so that at the end of the war there were in all 140 of the Type XXI U-boats ready for service (20 in Norwegian harbors and another 120 in Germany), while, of Type XXIII, 61 had been completed and a considerable number were already on patrol in British coastal waters. In the circumstances of that time, the numbers produced represented a really remarkable achievement, even though a considerable part of German industry, especially in the electrical trades, had been diverted from other tasks to attain it.

The Type XXI U-boats were constructed on two storys, in the lower of which was fitted a single, gigantic battery as the main source of power. On one charging, it could supply a submerged speed of 5 knots for slightly under four days, or, alternatively, a maximum speed of 16 knots for sixty minutes. In neither case was it necessary for the U-boat to surface or snort at periscope depth to renew the air.

The Type XXIII U-boats had a maximum submerged speed of thirteen knots. By snorting with the Diesel, both types could fully recharge their batteries in a matter of a few hours.

These U-boats contained many other new features. Their

torpedo compartments were much broader than in the old U-boats, and with their multifarious equipment they looked like engineering workshops on shore. Whereas previously the torpedo compartment had served as living space for part of the crew, in view of the strain of long underwater patrols, the torpedomen were now provided with separate quarters.

Much new equipment was also provided. To defeat the enemy radar, a skin of synthetic rubber now covered the top of the Snort, making it practically immune from detection, while a search receiver, working on the principle of the tuned dipole, was provided which reacted to the 9-centimeter waves of the British radar and gave warning when the U-boat was in the beam. The aerial of this apparatus was attached to the Snort mast.

Besides acoustic torpedoes, the Types XXI and XXIII U-boats carried a new type, the Lut. Whereas previously torpedoes could not be fired at an angle of more than 90 degrees to their target, these could be fired from any point on the compass and would set their own course to the target, making toward it in a series of wide, sweeping turns. Six of these torpedoes could be fired by a Type XXI U-boat in one salvo, after ten minutes a further six, and a third salvo after a period of half an hour—all from a depth of 160 feet.

In the autumn of 1944 the first three Type XXI boats to be completed were tested under operational conditions in the Baltic by two experienced U-boat commanders, Korvettenkapitän Emmermann and Fregattenkapitän Topp. They devised new tactics for both this and the smaller Type XXIII U-boat and laid down the principles on which crews were to be trained.

But, though production was meanwhile going ahead a great many teething troubles had yet to be overcome before the new U-boats could be made operational, and it was not until the beginning of May, 1945, that Korvettenkapitän Schnee was given command of the first Type XXI U-boat to be sent on patrol, the U.2511.

Here again, to save time, a stage in the normal process from drawing-board to active service was to be omitted and in the course of attacks on shipping in the Caribbean, he was told to make the fullest demands on his craft so that any further weakness or deficiencies that came to light could be rectified with the minimum of delay. In the event, the capitu-

lation came before he had got further than the Faroes and he
was ordered to return to Norway.

A few hours after the end of the second world war, Schnee
came upon his first "enemy" ship, a British cruiser. He went
through the drill of an attack and at least, then, before he
surrendered, he had the satisfaction of knowing that the new
U-boat performed according to plan.

The discussion of these technical developments, which, with
the Walter-boat and a new type of back-thrust torpedo powered on the same principle, were either in service or shortly to
be employed at the end of the war, raises the question whether
they would have enabled the U-boats to achieve victory
if the German armies had not crumbled in the field. There is
no doubt that the German High Command hoped and believed that they would. Nevertheless, it seems highly improbable, for to mention only one of many adverse factors, when
the end of the war came, the Allies had already for some
time been building merchant ships at the rate of a million
tons a month, and not since the end of 1942 had the rate at
which tonnage was sunk by the U-boats exceeded the rate at
which it could be replaced.

Command of Men in a U-Boat

Lecture

given in 1943 at a German Naval Officers' Course
by
Kapitän z.S. Wolfgang Lüth

Wolfgang Lüth was one of the most successful U-boat
commanders. In fourteen patrols, between January, 1940,
and October, 1943, he sank close on 250,000 gross tons
of shipping and in this period he spent over 600 days at
sea, setting up a record with 203 days on one patrol in
the Indian Ocean. He was holder of the Knight's Cross of
the Iron Cross, with Oak-Leaves, Swords and Brilliants.

MY TASK as a U-boat commander is to sink ships. To succeed in this task I need a crew to help me, and if they are to
be of any help they must not only be efficient in the perform-

ance of the innumerable daily jobs in a U-boat at sea, but they must enjoy doing them.

The Life of a Submariner

Life on board has long periods of monotony and one has to learn to endure lack of success for weeks on end. When this is accompanied by depth charges, a nervous strain is added which bears principally on the commander.

The man being depth-charged in a U-boat is in a similar situation to an airman being attacked, shall we say, by three fighters at once. Both can hear every individual "shot" that is being fired and the sound makes them shrink whether or not the shot strikes home.

But the U-boat man cannot fly away; he cannot move nor return the fire. Often, too, the lights in the U-boat go out under depth charging, and in the dark everyone feels more afraid.

Moreover, life in a U-boat is unnatural and unhealthy compared with service afloat. There is no sharp distinction between night and day, because inside the hull the lights have to be kept permanently burning. Weekdays and Sundays are indistinguishable and there is no regular alternation of the seasons. So the normal rhythm of life is disturbed and reduced to an even monotony, and it is the commander's job to do what he can to supply variety in its place.

Then, too, even the fittest and healthiest of the crew suffer under the perpetual change of climate encountered during patrol. The boat passes from the trade winds to the tropics, from damp and cold into the atmosphere of summer—one climatic zone after another.

Then, as a U-boat does most of her fighting at night, there is the question of irregular sleep, and on top of that, for the commander, the burden of his responsibility, lasting for weeks and keeping him continually at the highest pitch.

The fog on board gets on your nerves as well, the perpetual din, the movement of the boat—all this can produce the so-called "caneurosis." The effects of drinking strong coffee and too much smoking are bad for the stomach and nerves, particularly at night on an empty stomach. I have seen young lads of twenty-three, after two years of it, become unfit for seagoing service.

And of course one can't afford to get drunk too often
ashore—in wartime, at any rate. On patrol I have never drunk
the middle-watch coffee that is so popular in the Service. I
loathe the taste of it, myself, because it's made too strong. I
have never smoked more than one or two cigars a day and
I've never got drunk ashore—well, hardly ever. . . .

Morale of the Crew

The morale of the crew depends on:
   (1) Discipline.
   (2) The commander's success. Crews will always prefer
the successful commander, even though he may be a fat-
head, to the one who is consideration itself, but sinks no
ships.
   (3) A well-organized daily routine.
   (4) Officers who deal correctly with the men and set
them a good example.
   (5) A commander whose leadership embraces all aspects, mental, physical and spiritual, of his men's welfare.

Discipline

It is up to the commander to insure that the tone in the
seamen's mess is set by the right men and not the wrong ones.
He must be like a gardener—cultivate and encourage the
healthy plants and root out the weeds. That is not hard to
achieve, either, because we get mostly young men in the U-
boats, the ratings from twenty to twenty-two and the petty
officers usually between twenty-three and twenty-five. And it
helps here if you can have as many men as possible who have
learned some skilled trade in peacetime and if you have none,
preferably, of those half-educated youths who only completed
half their time at secondary school, either because they had
decided they'd had enough of their teachers or the other way
round.

My crews have come from all over Germany. The majority
of my petty officers have been married men, or engaged and
about to marry, and I find myself that married men are an
advantage. I know that women can undermine a soldier's
morale and will to fight, but I also know from my own experience that they can strengthen it. I have often noticed that

it was the married men who seemed to have benefited most from their leave. I was glad to have an opportunity once on leave of entertaining some of the wives and getting to know them. I told them what was expected of them and I think it helped them.

Obviously some of the punishments laid down in the disciplinary code cannot be applied to a U-boat in war, curtailment of leave, for example. Others, such as cells or stoppage of pay have little point. Suppose I gave a sailor 14 days' detention—he could not serve it, in any case, until the end of the patrol, so we would go on sharing the same dangers and the same successes until finally we were home again—all of us in high spirits, with the feeling of something achieved. And am I expected then, months after the offense, to send the man off to the glasshouse? I should think myself very foolish if I did.

But I continue at sea with C.O.'s reports and in serious cases all my officers attend. Suppose somebody was up for answering back a superior, something that would cost him normally three days' cells. I give him, instead, three days' hard lying—that means he sleeps on the bare deck without mattress or blanket: it is unpleasant, and it is more effective than cells.

Every punishment you give, of course, must be officially announced to the crew—you can put it in the ship's newspaper, or on the notice board, or if serious enough, you can call a muster. But any kind of victimization of the offender must be stamped on and you, the commander, must never let the man feel you are holding it against him. He must continue to feel he is liked, basically, and respected as one who pulls his weight with the rest.

In general, I tried to punish as little as I could. But that cannot be done by folding your hands and hoping for the best. You won't get away with it. You *must* be really concerned for the welfare of your men, have their interests at heart, and you must be determined to give them a lead and make something out of them. And, finally, when you give them orders, make it clear what you want them to do, so that they will be *able* to obey.

It should be clear that the commander should take care to be approachable and even-tempered at all times, otherwise, if

he holds himself aloof and shows resentment at being disturbed, sooner or later he will miss some vital piece of information.

Putting the Men "in the Picture"

In submarines, the crew labor under the disadvantage of
not being able to participate actively in an attack; all powers
of decision and initiative rest with the commander. At the
same time, it only needs a single mistake on the part of one
man—forgetting, say, to shut one valve before opening another—and the attack is ruined. Mistakes like that come
quickly to roost, but when everyone has done his job well and
as a result we manage to sink a ship, the men are only able to
share in the success at second hand. And so when there are
successes, the commander must do all he can—circumstances,
of course, permitting—to let the men see something of their
achievement.

Once, for example, in the middle of the night I came un-
expectedly on a convoy. Having nearly collided with one
destroyer, I managed to slip past another and get in an attack
on the ships. The visibility was poor, the situation confused,
so I went to half speed, till I could sort things out. After I had
given the necessary orders, I called down to the chief, who
was in the control room, and gave him the rough outline of
what was going on, so that he could tell the crew over the
loudspeakers. Then before I turned for the run-out, I told
them: "Am starting the attack," and when the fish had been
fired that it would be forty seconds at least before anything
happened.

Of course they all began counting. Number one started
easing the cork from the victory bottle and the triumphal
march was got out ready for the gramophone.

After two minutes' waiting when nothing had happened, I
closed the proceedings with the customary expressive mono-
syllable!

If you have sunk a ship and you are being depth-charged
afterward that is usually a good opportunity to tell the men
something more about the attack. If you have the luck to be
able to stay on the surface, you can let one or two come up
to the bridge to see the steamer as she is sinking; or, at periscope-depth, they can have a look through the lens.

Security

"The only things worth hearing are the things you're not supposed to be told"—that's a common belief among Germans, I know: it is among my crews. So on our last patrol, while we were still in the Bay, on our way back to base, I dived deep and spoke to the men about security. I not only told them what they could *not* say but tried to show them some of the things that *could* be told, that people would still find worth hearing.

Afterward I put up a specimen letter on the notice-board:

Dear Erika, am home safe again. We have had some fine successes and have sunk a few steamers. We even sank a shark. I won first prize in the chess tournament.

I added a whole list of things they could mention about the patrol, so they could pick out what applied to themselves.

Making the Most of U-boat Life

If men are to settle down in a U-boat and come to look on it as their home—as they do, after a time—their daily life must be organized on a sound and permanent basis—but not over-organized. When he is off duty, a sailor's time is his own and it is his undisputed right to be left in peace.

As night and day on board a U-boat tend to merge and become confused, the commander must do what he can to restore the distinction artificially. During supper, for example, I have the lights dimmed throughout the boat, and for an hour afterward every evening we have a concert on gramophone records. The watch is changed at 20.00 and the concert runs for half an hour before and half an hour after, with an interval between.

The difference between Sunday and weekdays is also underlined. We start Sunday with a concert and the first record is always the same: "Till ten o'clock it's my Sunday treat to stay in bed and rest my feet . . . ," and the last record of the day is also the same, but something better: "Abendlied," sung by the choirboys of Regensburg Cathedral.

I like too, to see the men make a special effort in their dress on Sundays. I tell them: "If any of you have still got a clean shirt and want to show it off sometime, then don't waste it on a weekday—let's see it on Sunday."

At the start of a patrol each man brings a dozen or so magazines and illustrated papers on board and I dole them out a few at a time. There are always enough to hand out six new ones on Sundays, and on the last day of the patrol there is still usually one left.

The heads situation can give some difficulty, when you have new hands in the crew who don't know how to work the pump properly. So that they won't keep everybody waiting, I have a notice put up on the wall: BE BRIEF! I have a notebook hung in the heads, as well, in which every "caller" must enter his name. Then if there's a blockage I seize on the last-named and make him pump until it is cleared. So that it shall seem less like confessing a crime, everyone can add some little verse after his name, if he wants. We get so many by the end of a patrol, you could almost fill a whole evening reciting them!

Meals

It is a difficult thing to draw up the menu; somebody is going to bleat, whatever you do. So I let each mess decide for themselves what they are going to eat, with the proviso that they don't eat up all the good things first. On long patrols, of course, you have got to start rationing fairly soon.

I make a point of seeing that the men are properly dressed when they sit down to a meal, including the petty officers; not because I am an aesthete, but because their authority suffers if they don't keep themselves up to the mark. Yet I have seen petty officers laying into a messman because a plate had a smear on it, while one of them had such greasy hands he was dirtying everything he touched. This kind of inconsistency can lead to endless bad feeling and it is quite easy to avoid. The ideal to aim at is that complaints should only be made when there really is something to complain about.

Medical Treatment

We have never held sick parade on board: with a fit crew, I think it's unnecessary. But I have taught the men to come to

the doctor or to me even for small things, not with the object
of making them soft or encouraging them to malinger, but so
that they shall stay fit. It is better for a boil to be treated in
the early stages rather than the man should feel ashamed to
report it and wait till it looks more impressive.

Some points of hygiene: I make it an express order that
everyone must wear a belly band and I remind the whole crew
about it each evening over the loudspeaker before it gets dark.
No one may drink iced water in the tropics. The young sailors
are forbidden to smoke on an empty stomach, and I see to it
that the middle-watch coffee is not as strong as it is usually
made in the Service.

We have never had any sexual problems, even on the long-
est patrol. But I do not permit the men to cover the sides of
their bunks with pictures of naked women. Because you are
hungry, it doesn't mean that you've got to draw loaves of
bread on the walls. It is a good thing, too, to glance occasionally through the books on board, you will always find something that appeals to the baser instincts and it is better overboard.

When we go ashore, I encourage the men to buy as much
as possible for their families, so as to make sure they spend
their money sensibly. But when they are back at base they
must be allowed to let themselves go a bit, too.

The Officers

The spirit of the ship's company depends to a great extent
on the example which is set by the officers. So far I have had
seventeen under my command. Four of them were not really
suited to the U-boat Service but finally managed to adapt
themselves, seven were midshipmen, and of these one was a
failure. All the others were good and helped to make life on
board what it should be, "every day a Sunday."

With the young officers, you must take some trouble. It's
clear they are all different, but in case you should forget it,
they sometimes go out of their way to underline the fact.

On a long patrol in a small ship like a U-boat you can't
allow any smut or filthy stories in the wardroom, not only
because it is against morality generally, but because once
started such things are liable to get out of hand, and above
all because of the example which it sets the men.

I often talk with the officers when they are doing duty-watch on the bridge. I ask them what sort of avoiding action should we take today, in the conditions prevailing, if we suddenly encounter destroyers? If aircraft are sighted, when ought we to dive and when can we stay on the surface? When will be the best time for attack, and from which side? I discuss the situation with them in the light of the charts and let them make suggestions—but they must be positive suggestions, inspired by the attacking spirit, for of fear I have plenty myself without any help from others.

Certainly, you must leave the officers to themselves sometimes in the wardroom, so that they can have a good, hearty bellyache at their commander. Meals are taken together, of course, and everyone must be properly dressed: we have a white, or once-white bed sheet as tablecloth. For a civilized life, the daily game of cards is essential—Doppelkopf usually—and it is pleasant if a book can go the rounds and we can discuss it together afterward.

Depth Charges

It has been said so often, it's become a platitude: when you're being depth-charged, everyone looks to the officers. I had one officer—he was off-duty watch at the time—who actually went to sleep once during a depth-charging! He didn't wake up until some fittings came adrift and landed on his head, then all he did was to give a sort of peevish grunt, mutter something about "restless times" and immediately doze off again. When we surfaced, we got caught in a mine field and I asked him whether he thought we ought to keep more to port or to starboard. He gave the guileless answer: "Doesn't matter, really. If you wake up tomorrow, you'll know you were right, that's all." He wasn't being awkward; he was just placid by nature, with a kind of dry humor.

Besides the officers, the chief burden when you are being depth-charged falls on the seaman at the hydrophones, because he can hear the approaching destroyer before anyone else. I never allow him in any circumstances to call out to me the H.E. bearings direct. Every report is passed to me by a communications number, a quiet man with a quiet voice. And he never uses the word destroyer, that's taboo; we speak

of a "small vessel" so that the men won't be needlessly
alarmed.

You must manage somehow during depth-charging to get
the men off watch to lie down and sleep and you must make
sure that they are really breathing through their potash cartridges—the officers, as well—because they are uncomfortable
and the men tend to dodge using them when they think no
one's looking. Then when everything has been done it is as
well for the commander himself to lie down as though for
sleep. The men like to see that, because they take it as a sign
that things are not too bad, after all. But first I go through
the boat and tell them what we are doing to put the enemy
off the scent; that's imporant, you must not forget that, when
you get a chance.

Morale

During a long patrol the officers must show imagination
and resource and the men must remain capable of responding
eagerly when they are given a lead. I prefer, myself, not to be
the prime mover in arranging off-duty activities. I simply talk
over possibilities with the officers and men, make a suggestion
or two and then leave the rest to them.

Chess and Skat tournaments are easy to organize. We
broadcast the state of the rounds and put them in the ship's
newspaper, and for the first two or three times enthusiasm
lasts well.

The men must know what they are fighting for and they
must consciously and willingly stake their lives for it. In
many, a somewhat passive attitude has to be overcome. On
Sundays, sometimes, I dive deep and hold a general muster
of the crew. I tell them, then, something of the Reich and the
centuries-old struggle to achieve it and in this setting I talk to
them about the great figures of our history and the contribution which they have made.

I get the officers to deliver lectures on subjects in which
they are interested: the chief, for example, on the use of coal
as a raw material; someone else on the Atlantic, its climate,
and animal life, on the Gulf Stream, Trade Winds, flying-fish
—all things which should be part of a seamen's general
knowledge.

Such lectures help to provide topics for the men to discuss

in their free time and when the subject has been presented to them in their own language they will often go on discussing it for days, for most of his spare time the U-boat man spends lying on his bunk, chinning with his friends.

As in most U-boats, we have our own newspaper. It always starts with short extracts from the political news and I consider this part so important, I always compile it myself. The second part is devoted to local news, that is to say the events of the last few days, dealt with in a humorous way. Always particularly appreciated have been the items, BdU-News and the Radio Press, which together provide such a good picture of the general situation.

Before the start of a patrol, you must make sure that enough books are on board and that there is a sufficient variety, solid books as well as the lighter kind. There is a small point in this connection. The men are fond of reading, but you cannot expect them, when they have been standing for hours on watch, to sit reading in a poor light at a more or less wobbly messtable, wedged in between spare torpedoes and other gear. They want to lie down in comfort for a change, and it is quite easy to make small lamps on board, one for each bunk, so that they can read as well, if they want to.

However many gramophone records you have on board, by the end of a long patrol you are tired of them all. So I allow only an hour's music each day and let the messes choose the program in turn so that there is something to suit all tastes. When it is somebody's birthday, he's allowed to choose the whole program himself.

I have already mentioned the Skat and Chess Tournaments. We have had other competitions, too; for example, each man had to sing a song through the microphone and the whole crew awarded marks, as at school. As first prize, the winner was excused a duty-watch and the commander had to do it for him. As second prize, if the winner was a seaman, he was allowed to start the Diesels under the supervision of an E.R.A., and if he came from the engine room, he was allowed to come up to the bridge and take command of the boat for a while.

Then we got up a sporting contest, with running commentary on the "radio" and cheering masses of spectators, after the style of the Olympic Games. A length of cord with a heavy weight on the end was attached to a stick about eighteen inches long. The stick had to be held upright and worked with the wrists until the cord had twisted itself round it to the end. The winner was the one who could wind the weight up and down the stick the greatest number of times. I am describing these things in some detail to show you that there are endless ways of arranging amusements for the men in a U-boat.

We also laid on a tall story contest. Everyone had to think up some fabulous story of his adventures, of the kind men on leave tell to their families, and relate it over the microphone to the ship's company. Some of the lies were really good, up to the standard, almost, of those you see in print!

I will give one last example. The medical officer had been instructing the men in health and hygiene. So that we could do something sitting down, for a change, we arranged a poetry competition. Everyone had to compose a four- or eight-line verse conveying in humorous form some point which the doctor had made.

Now two things are essential, if you are to have success in a U-boat. The first is discipline. The second is the most sustained and rigorous training of the crew in the smallest details of their duties. This is a well-known axiom and I will not enlarge on it. But there is another thing—and I have dealt in some detail with these spare-time activities in order to illustrate it—namely, the commander must show a real and active concern for the welfare of his men. It is not enough for him to issue orders and hand out punishments from time to time, for he is absolutely dependent for success on the men wanting the same things as himself. Both must live for their boat and for nothing else, and the men must be happy to sail in her under that and no other commander.

I will give an example which will show what I mean.

I had on one patrol a coxswain who was a nice enough fellow, but had an unfortunate tendency to get rattled. We were making our way through one of our own minefields and I told him: "Tomorrow morning, at 03.00, you must begin to zig-zag, because it will be starting to get light then and we may encounter enemy submarines. Tomorrow morning at 05.00, we will alter course from 300 to 270."

When I got to the bridge at five next morning, I found that he had already altered course without me—two hours before, at the same time as he had started to zigzag! After steering for a while on 270, he had then confused port with starboard and gone to 240 for his next leg, instead of to 300. So for two full hours, we had been snaking our way through the middle of a minefield.

It was a horrible sensation and infuriating to think we might have gone sky-high through a shambles like that. I couldn't refrain from telling him that if we struck a mine, I'd have it in for him in heaven! We turned immediately and made our way back carefully, following the same route.

Now if he gets blown to smithereens, what good does it do the commander, in a situation like that, to say to himself, "It wasn't my fault?" No. Let him not waste time apportioning blame; let him take care to do all he should, in future, to prevent such things happening again. He needn't worry about unpleasant surprises—there'll be plenty of them, anyway.

The commander and his officers can and must see to it that mistakes of this kind are reduced as nearly as possible to zero, for if things go wrong it is they, in the last resort, who are to blame. I am convinced that many a U-boat has been lost through errors even smaller than this and that many a boat has been robbed of success through equally unpredictable and incalculable shortcomings.

Do not forget: it is the duty of the commander to have faith in his men and to be determined to go on trusting them despite sometimes being let down. For we have one great advantage: our young men are unreservedly eager and ready to come to grips with the enemy and, so long as they are led with revolutionary ardor, they will glady return, again and again, to the attack. But we must respect them and we must like them.

German U-Boat Types

Type	Surface Displacement	Surface Speed	Submerged Speed
IA	862 tons	17¾ knots	8.3 knots
II	250 tons	13 knots	6.9 knots
VII	600 to 1,000 tons	16 to 17 knots	8 knots
IX	740 tons	18 knots	7.3 to 7.7 knots
IXD/1	1,610 tons	16.5 knots	6.9 knots
IXD/2	1,616 tons	19.2 knots	6.9 knots
XIV	1,688 tons	14.4 knots	6.2 knots
XIX	Projected Supply Type: none completed		
XX	Ditto		
XXI	1,620 tons	15.6 knots	17 knots
XXIII	230 tons	9.7 knots	12 knots
XXVI	The 'Walter' U-boat, still experimental at the end of the war.		

Ships Sunk by German U-Boats

No authoritative figures are available from any source of shipping tonnage sunk by German U-boats alone, as distinct from Axis and Japanese U-boats combined.

Unofficial assessments have been published in Germany of German U-boats' sinkings and weekly and monthly figures of shipping lost through enemy action in general are, of course, available in a number of British and United States official publications.

In cases where individual ships are known to have been sunk by German U-boats, their tonnage is given in the text as "gross register tonnage," that is, the measurement expressed in hundreds of cubic feet of all the enclosed spaces in the ship.

"Gross register tonnage" is usually more than the "Light Displacement tonnage" (the weight of the ship, minus stores, water, etc., as she leaves the builder's yard), but, in the case of cargo ships, considerably less than the "loaded displacement tonnage," i.e. the weight of the ship, plus the weight of all she can carry on the draft to which her Plimsoll mark allows her to be submerged.

The numbers of ships sunk by German U-boats, given on another page, are based on German estimates.

German post-war assessment of British, Allied and Neutral ships destroyed in all areas (Atlantic, Mediterranean and Indian Ocean) by German U-Boats:

	1939	1940	1941	1942	1943	1944	1945
January		40	21	47	35	12	11
February		43	38	69	58	15	15
March		23	41	82	100	21	12
April		7	43	66	46	9	13
May		13	58	120	44	4	3
June		58	61	119	15	10	—
July		38	22	85	44	11	—
August		56	23	101	16	17	—
September	40	59	51	91	18	7	—
October	27	63	30	86	17	—	—
November	13	32	12	106	9	6	—
December	24	37	17	55	9	9	—

1939:1940:1941:1942:1943:1944:1945:

	1939	1940	1941	1942	1943	1944	1945	
Total No. of ships:	104	469	417	1027	411	121	54	=2,003 ships

Numbers of German U-Boats at Sea and Numbers Destroyed —Monthly Figures

Example: Under September 1939, "2/23" means 2 destroyed out of an average of 23 at sea during that month. The latter figures refer to the Atlantic Ocean only.

Year	Jan.	Feb.	Mar.	Apr.	May	June	July	Aug.	Sept.	Oct.	Nov.	Dec.
1939									2/23	5/10	1/16	1/8
1940	2/11	5/15	1/13	5/24	1/8	0/18	2/11	3/13	0/13	1/12	2/11	0/10
1941	0/8	0/12	5/13	2/19	1/24	4/32	1/27	3/36	2/36	2/36	5/38	10/25
1942	3/42	2/50	6/48	3/49	4/61	3/59	12/70	9/86	10/100	16/105	13/95	5/97
1943	6/92	19/116	15/116	15/111	41/118	17/86	37/84	25/59	9/60	26/86	19/78	8/67
1944	15/66	20/68	25/68	21/57	22/43	25/47	23/34	34/50	24/68	12/45	19/78	32/51
1945	12/39	22/47	34/56	37/54	28/45						8/41	

The most fascinating people and events of World War II